To Hell with Male Prostitutes and other stories

by

Venansio Ahabwe

RoseDog  Books

PITTSBURGH, PENNSYLVANIA 15238

RoseDog Books
585 Alpha Drive Suite 103
Pittsburgh, PA 15238
Visit our website at *www.rosedogbookstore.com*

ISBN: 978-1-4349-3084-2
eISBN: 978-1-4349-7152-4

Venansio Ahabwe (M.A. SSPM, B Ed, Dip Ed, Dip Emp. Law)

To Hell with Male Prostitutes
and other stories
A unique inquiry into our day-to-day beliefs

'To Hell with Male Prostitutes *and other stories' is a collection of editorial pieces, selected from hundreds of articles, authored by Venansio Ahabwe and published in newspapers. The stories appeared in 'Peering Eye' and 'The Comrade' columns in Tanzania's Sunday Citizen and Guardian on Sunday respectively, as well as Uganda's Monitor, New Vision, and Observer. Media reports of occurring events provided raw material for the largely comic answers in this text. Prostitution is considered an immoral, feminine activity in the ordinary sense. The possibility of male prostitutes therefore suggests a risk of extreme social depravity that may thrive amidst socially approved conduct. It challenges the reader to always think beyond 'normal' meanings. Written in simple style, this book is ideal for mental relaxation and can also be used in school for language and literature studies. Much of the content borders on the ludicrous, with jokes and near-phobic wit to mock conventional human beliefs and manners – Author.*

Contents

Part 1: FAIRNESS, MORALITY, AND ETHICS

1. Death penalty is inhuman! It denies us the opportunity to forgive.

A woman was nearly killed by her master. In self-defence, she wrested a gun from him and shot him dead instead. Very soon, she was charged with murder, tried, sentenced to death and executed immediately. Her family and descendants later took up the matter, arguing that she deserved to be pardoned. It has now been realised that the punishment she got was disproportionately harsh; therefore she has been forgiven posthumously, sixty years after her death.

In case this is news to you, the media has reported a 1945 incident of the only woman ever executed in Georgia's electric chair. She was a black woman named Lena Baker, who was sentenced to die after appearing before a marathon one-day trial by an all-white, all-male jury. During her brief trial, she had testified that a man, E. B. Knight, whom she had been hired to care for, had held her against her will in a gristmill and threatened to shoot her if she tried to leave. She then grabbed Knight's gun and shot him when he raised a metal bar to strike her.

Now, the Georgia Board of Pardons and Paroles has decided to absolve Lena Baker, noting that she was not innocent, but the decision to deny her clemency in 1945 "was a grievous error". The Georgia-based prison-advocacy group, Prison and Jail Project, assisted Baker's descendants with the pardon request; whereupon the project director John Cole Vodicka described Baker's murder as a "blatant instance of injustice … a legal lynching".

It is unreasonable to punish a criminal by killing him, as it is strange to forgive a dead person after killing him. In Baker's case, after the Board's decision, her grandnephew, who led the family's effort to clear her name, consoled thus: "I believe she's somewhere around God's throne and can look down and smile."

Nevertheless, this scenario brings to light the folly and danger of terminating human life presumably in the administration of justice. The existence of capital punishment on a country's statute books is a bad mark on the society's perception of justice and disfigures its reputation before man, God, or both.

Only a month ago, Tanzanian politicians, human rights activists, and prominent lawyers called on government to scrape the death sentence from the country's law books and substitute it with life imprisonment. Unfortunately, not all of them were unanimous that capital punishment is primarily bad and inhuman, but many argued that it is no longer worth the paper it is written on because "not a single death sentence has been effected, ... no president has endorsed any, ... and convicts never get hanged". ('Lawyers: Repeal death penalty' *Sunday Citizen* 24th July 2005).

One finds the arguments advanced by most commentators quite disagreeable as the major reason they are denouncing capital punishment in Tanzania is because it has not been implemented in reality. It has remained on paper, so it is discouraged apparently for swelling up the pages of the law-books. To retain it is to waste paper space. In addition, the number of the would-be-hanged convicts is causing congestion in prisons, and thus inconveniencing the criminals who do not deserve death. Else, it would be appropriate for convicted persons to be hanged regularly and urgently, purposely to decongest the cells.

The solution to the death penalty would mainly be to sensitise ourselves of the fact that it is a violation of human rights, as life is the greatest gift from the Creator, befitting both the holy and sinful humans alike. One would concur with Dr. Sengondo Mvungi and Prof. Ibrahim Lipumba – acknowledging that hanging a transgressor is not a deterrent to crimes; therefore besides holding a national debate on the death penalty, research should be carried out to determine what makes people kill, and devise an equable conclusion.

A dead wrongdoer cannot repent and be reformed to be useful to self and the community, which should be the crucial purpose of punishment. The hanging of a reprobate does not compensate the offended party, apart from giving a wild sense of relief through revenge. Sometimes, a suspect might be falsely accused, and when this comes to light after his death, no amount of human effort could repair the damage. Moreover, no offence makes anyone of us so inhuman as to deserve death because "an eye for an eye would make the whole world blind".

By Venansio Ababwe, published in Sunday Citizen, Dar es Salaam, 21st August, 2005

2. Saddam Hussein laughs at death

The year 2006 was the worst in the brief history of my life, because it ended with all media houses relaying awful images of a human body, dangling in a rope that had been loosened round Saddam Hussein's neck, wringing him to death. The portrait of the flaccid corpse was a terrible sight, and Peering Eye considers that whoever committed this blunder is nothing but a terrorist!

Shockingly, once Saddam had been hanged, an American politician called the act a "milestone in the history of Iraq". What a folly! Some people even held street celebrations: well, it is not strange that human beings can rejoice at the murder of a fellow human. How that sort of 'joy' comes about, only psychiatrists can explain! However as his killers celebrated and thumped their chests, the victim must have laughed at their impudence, knowing that soon or later, they too would follow him as he followed those he was accused of killing.

Peering Eye would never have participated in such a heartless dance; I would rather have urged my executioner to hang me than become so bestial. The slaughter of Saddam Hussein was a pointless deed; cursed be its architects. Man can never be a total devil or a pure angel, and thus Saddam must have been as good as he was bad: probably like you and me. Far from imputing that Saddam was innocent, I ask the reader to remember that he was not a gang leader being showered with bullets as he shot back from his hide-out. He was not on the run either.

Guilty as he was, handcuffed, Saddam Hussein was led to the gallows, a noose placed around his neck and he was left to hang. Need I say that Saddam's death further illustrates the vainness of death as a punishment? True, many people lost their loved ones during the dictator's reign, but if we are to look for what Iraq and humanity will benefit from the execution of this criminal, there is nothing but emotional satisfaction to the families he wronged and the politicians he opposed. Sheer revenge!

Once upon a time in 1945, Italian dictator Benito Amilcare Andrea Mussolini attempted to escape the advancing Allied Army but he was captured and executed along with 15 leading Fascists on April 29, 1945. Their bodies were hung vengefully: - also as a lesson to future dictators. But alas and alack, Europe has since produced Slobodan Milosevic and brutal dictators lurk in almost every continent till this day.

The moral is that the death penalty is neither a form of justice nor a solution to crime. It might not be strange to realise that the crime of misgoverning a nation cannot possibly have been limited to Saddam Hussein. Many world presidents commit it often in diverse styles; which is why many presidents strive to keep in power too long. If death was the most appropriate penalty, then every defeated President would deserve hanging.

The hanging of Saddam Hussein might also show that Shakespeare was absolutely right. He said, "The evil that men do lives after them; the good is interred with their bones; ... men have lost their reason!" (*Julius Caesar* Act 3, Scene 2, line 75 – 100).

Peering Eye knows well that to mourn Saddam is unacceptable, even punishable in some places but the folly is that suppose he was not hanged, still he would have to die some day. He was always destined to die like you and I.

The only shock about his death is that he looked his executioners straight in the eye and appeared to persuade them to fulfil their mission (to hang him) with ease. Besides, he has died as one among hundreds of thousands of Iraqis who continue to die consequent upon the invasion of their country by the Coalition Forces. He is another victim of a military misadventure. To mourn his death is fitting, whereas to rejoice could only amuse him like those he killed must have chuckled when he followed them

By Venansio Ahabwe, published in Sunday Citizen, Dar es Salaam, 7th January 2007

3. Pornography is in every house. Police need not investigate.

This is to abide by the Dar es Salaam Special Zone Police Commander, Mr Alfred Tibaigana's directive issued recently that everyone associated with pornographic literature should submit themselves to police before they are arrested. It may be still fresh in your mind how some guys, including a couple, were picked like litter and thrown in police coolers for the comical allegation that they were "publishing and distributing pornographic publications".

Mr. Tibaigana announced the capture of the wretched pornographic souls with such enthusiasm; you would think he had captured Bin Laden and was announcing it to the American public before leading him to the White House for a chat with George Bush. But once he asked the public to stop buying and consuming pornographic products, which promotes their publication and sale, Mr. Tibaigana acknowledged that the public enjoys pornography.

Why did he jail the pornographic persons then if they were acting on popular demand? Well, Peering Eye may think Alfred was wrong but, being incapable of bringing the Commander to account, let me volunteer more clues that might lead to further arrests.

Arrest Peering Eye! Why? The story you are reading now is pornographic material. Both the author and the reader are now guilty. Even Mr. Tibaigana should be reported if he reads it. I am even sure the police feasted on the magazines they seized, or how did they confirm they were indeed pornographic? They should have been arrested there and then.

Secondly, police may visit Peering Eye's residence and peep through the window onto the wide screen in the corner of his seating-room. They will break into the house to arrest everyone, or order the entire house bombed down, just to rid Africa of 'one evil man'! Yes, the screen images that will greet their eyes will be so redolent; any 'functional man' would not walk away unstrapped.

Anyhow, police must not merely look for Peering Eye's house, whose location we cannot disclose now. Random spot-checks at any quarters inhabited by a young man or woman – even some journalists who attended Alfred's briefing – will simply produce a criminal. Pornographic movies are gaining unrivalled status on the family menu, and many of us are latent convicts on that account.

Have you not seen vendors of visual compact discs (VCDs) and other similar paraphernalia? Did police ever check their stocks? Is pornography solely circulated through magazines? You may imagine so if your understanding of the concept is limited.

Pornography is the public depiction of erotic behaviour intended to cause sexual excitement – using pictures, sound, gestures, and etcetera.

It is any behaviour that communicates via speech, body language, publication, entertainment, broadcast, pictorial, motion, fashion, literature, a combination of some or all the above forms to show unclothed or under-clothed sexually arousing parts of a human body, such as thighs, buttocks, and genitalia.

That being so, need I illustrate to the police any more pornographic persons in town? Bwana Alfred, have you seen any half-naked persons in intense miniskirts? What about tight jeans? Who cares about the fulltime naked crowds at the beaches –all tribes of naked bodies, in shifting shapes and sizes. Would our musicians and dancers make momentous impressions without the dance strokes with sex innuendos?

Having revealed the vibrant scenes and incidences of pornography all over the nation, I think police will reward Peering Eye handsomely for reporting crime. It is incumbent on them to investigate these allegations, and apprehend all the public offenders since the aforementioned are common, public phenomena.

It is thus preposterous to arrest a few unknown fellows for possessing guarded pornographic magazines while all over the place there are pornographers doing their things without fear or suspicion. The context under which a few men and a woman were seized and incarcerated must be placed in the broader definition of "pornography" as a crime, to avoid misapprehension and confusion.

By Venansio Ahabwe, published in Sunday Citizen, Dar es Salaam Sunday 1st October 2006

---

4. Examination cheats must not be blamed

One day, a group of sinners ganged up against a woman, caught red-handed in the act of *usione soo*. When a wise man asked how many in the crowd would not have or had never done a similar thing given the opportunity, the stones they had wanted to throw at the adulterous woman dropped freely from their hands and the crowd melted into thin air.

Irksome reports of the current Form Four examinations leakage have hit media headlines with several disturbing revelations. *The Citizen* has described the cheating candidates as "hundreds of 'dishonest' From 4 candidates who have been sailing through the final national exams after accessing the question paper" ('Form 4 cheats celebrate', *The Citizen* 8th November 2004).

It is inconceivable how, ordinarily, a candidate would have fled from the examination suppliers. At the slightest suspicion of a topic from which a single examination question might be drawn, a student will naturally rummage through the entire chapter and cram the salient concepts. Let alone coming across the exact paper that might make or unmake their entire life!

The declaration by the Minister of Education and Culture Mr. Joseph Mungai that 'after verification of the truth, there is no way out, the examination in Dar es Salaam will be cancelled' is not pleasant at all. ('Form 4 exams in the balance' *The Citizen* 6th November 2004). Anyone who has ever taken an examination will understand how painful, if it were nullified and one required, to go through the hell of rigorous preparations to do the loathsome stuff again.

The intriguing question is, who cheated and who was actually cheated in these examinations? Did the candidates cheat or were they cheated? What about their parents, the schools, the Ministry of Education, National Examination Council of Tanzania (NECTA)? The Ministry and NECTA particularly cheated the candidates by supplying a raw deal to their clients, the candidates, and not doing everything necessary to prevent the leakage of the examinations. If we are to apportion blame for this mess, the candidates will honestly emerge less guilty. The bearers of the bigger blame, surely, should also take the bigger punishment.

A story is told of a woman in Kibaha who had sat awkwardly but ended up whipping her son for allowing his eye to stray and glance at her exposed genitalia. It is a curse! My God! It is impossible to control our eyes. By the time you know that you have seen what you are forbidden to see, you have already seen it.

Whoever released the examinations to the public, together with the sellers who worked to perpetrate the crime, deserve punishment. The students were mere victims of a lousy system that allowed the otherwise serious national matter to be profaned with impunity. The perpetrators therefore must not cover their guilt by crucifying the victims because the students deserved genuine examinations that would have been administered in an atmosphere of transparency and fairness, devoid of tension or infringement of rules.

The candidates missed the opportunity to be properly tested to express and prove themselves through a genuine and fair medium of academic assessment. This is a betrayal. It is frustrating to know that a candidate on the next desk or at the neighbouring examination centre is reproducing the answers they have rehearsed, even if the claim that only Geography leaked stands true.

Inevitably therefore, the 'fortunate' students had to celebrate, in which case "at one secondary school…Form 3 students were freely practicing a paper which turned out to be the next days Form 4 final paper" (*The Citizen* 8th November 2005).

All this boils down to a loophole in the school assessment methods, which should necessarily be progressive so that the best student can always come up, whatever the emergency. Else, how will the education authorities tell which grades the students deserve once the threat to cancel the examinations is carried through? What will be the criteria for spotting the guilty students?

At the same time, upholding the examinations as they have been is an injustice to the students who did not access the leaked papers. It is demoralising. It leads to loss of self-confidence to students in remote areas who learn of such urban developments. It is a disincentive to the poor pupils who know that as they do not have money to purchase final examinations, studying hard will not make a difference. Yet, the rich pupils could easily shun books, confident that money will deliver the results after all.

Compare the students' feelings in Dar es Salaam and Songea, Arusha and Karagwe, Dodoma and Kigoma. The leakage of examinations has inflicted serious damage not only on the institution charged with managing school examinations, but also on candidates' psychological and emotional standing. It is therefore necessary that the top authorities should clearly and immediately labour to repair the damage.

By Venansio Ahabwe, published in Sunday Citizen, Dar es Salaam 14th November 2004

5. David Banda, the African child taken by American parents

A thirteen-month baby, David Banda has been the axis of a recent fracas, soaking up worldwide media as regards whether he ought to have been given away to a well-to-do couple of the Western origin. The boy's mother, Marita died a month after she had given birth to him in their Mchinji village, in the Republic of Malawi. As a result David remained with his pitiable father, Yohanne Banda but was effectively looked after by a charity – Home of Hope Orphanage Centre – located at the Zambian boarder.

American born singer, Madonna has been on a goodwill mission to Africa that culminated in her ten-day excursion into Malawi where she has pledged about three million dollars to help almost a million orphans in the country. This was part of her operation to help the society to rout poverty and the ravages of HIV and Aids, which is a major reason the number of orphans is escalating.

Nonetheless, the well-heeled pop star's entire trip to Malawi has been reduced to a single adoption event, which has touched off a lively storm in the country. When Madonna decided to adopt the disconsolate infant named David, her decision drew significant commotion in Malawi and indeed African and the world. She was given an interim order for eighteen months to fly David to England where he would be periodically checked up by a London social worker, as court processed actual adoption orders for Madonna, jointly with her husband, Mr. Guy Ritchie.

This episode, however, would not pass uncontested. The Malawi human rights consultative committee of sixty-seven civil society organisations called the adoption illegal and sought a court injunction. They asserted that the adoption process has been "fast-tracked" to circumvent the law, which forbids foreigners from adopting Malawian children, if they have not lived in the country and been assessed for at least eighteen months.

Apparently, the protesting civil rights groups impressed it on the child's father that the adoption procedures had been flouted and that it could bring more serious repercussions for him and his child than what he had imagined. On Sunday 22nd October 2006, it was reported that Yohanne Banda, David Banda's father, had confessed he did not understand what adoption meant, and had not realised that he was giving up his child "for good".

Said Banda, "I was never told that adoption means that David will no longer be my son .... If I was told this, I would not have allowed the adoption.

A judge in Malawi has been working on a decision as whether charities have a right to a say in the adoption of one-year-old David.

It is interesting to note, however, that Yohanne Banda was later to turn around and support the adoption.

He said, "Nothing can make me change my mind," and blamed the 'so called human rights activists' for harassing him. He swore that he could never support the court case, knowing very well what he had agreed with Madonna and her husband.

Public opinion has been divided as a result. Some people have said that we have enough orphans and other suffering children to share with other persons of goodwill, Africans or non-Africans. It is argued that Madonna could have taken as many children as she wanted, if the intention was to care for and furnish them with essentials of life to grow normally into useful individuals. Madonna agrees strongly.

In an interview with *Time Magazine* on 5th November 2006, Madonna asked rather rhetorically, "Do you know how many children are going to die in the next two years? It's a stupid law" – one that required her to have stayed in Malawi for eighteen months to be eligible to adopt a child there.

'Adoption' is a way of providing a new family for a child when living with its own family is not possible. For many children, adoption may be their only chance of experiencing family life. After a successful adoption, returning a child to its parent(s) is impossible because an Adoption Order severs all legal ties with a child's birth family and confers parental rights and responsibilities on the new adoptive family. The birth parents no longer have any legal rights over the child and they are not entitled to claim them back. The child becomes a full member of the adopter's family, often taking their surname – David Banda has been renamed David Banda Mwale Ciccone Ritchie. The adopted child also assumes the same rights and privileges, including the right of inheritance, as if they had been born to the family.

This is the fact which the Malawian father of the adopted child has just woken up to. He has said, "I was never told that adoption means that David will no longer be my son... If I was told this, I would not have allowed the adoption."

The key concern in adoption is if the adopter can provide a stable home for a child until adulthood and beyond. Courts view adoption from the child's perspective – an adoption order will only be granted if it is viewed as being in the best interests of the child.

Was Madonna's adoption of David warranted? This writer believes that hers was a humane deed which was wrongly executed and might set a bad precedent. There are innumerable bighearted persons in the world but they cannot simply go about picking humans from their wretched habitats apparently to improve their conditions. The resultant uproar among the Malawi civil society organisations is only a response to the underhand games that were played in giving away Baby David. Once such an adoption is upheld, it might enable future criminals, like human traffickers, to seize their victims through legal procedures.

The human rights groups and other critics are concerned because Madonna appears to have skirted Malawian laws which have a residency requirement for prospective parents. They say that the three million dollar pledge that she made to the nation through her Raising Malawi charity appears to have shaped the government's behaviour. Critics are also concerned because fraudulent international adoptions are a lucrative business today

By Venansio Ahabwe, published in Child-Link Magazine Volume 11 No 3, Kampala December 2006

6. Compensate innocent prisoners

Of late, the country has been at crossroads because of the case involving suspects of the alleged People's Redemption Army (PRA). The judiciary went on strike along with lawyers. Politicians too got embroiled in nasty exchanges in parliament, cabinet and streets; sadly a child reportedly died in Kampala.

Nonetheless, some prisoners still remained undefended, even unnoticed, while they are not guilty. They are not essentially capable of committing the least of crimes nor can ever pass as possible suspects, but they stay jailed! They are children often imprisoned with their mothers. Precisely, Tendo who spent most of its babyhood in Luzira prison was quite a reminder and provoked this critique. ('Prisoners have sex on the bus' *The Weekly Observer* 22nd – 28th March 2007).

It does not matter whether Tendo's mother Ms. Betty Nambooze was guilty or innocent. The act of taking a baby prisoner merely because a parent is a convict or suspect is disturbing enough. To visit punishment on the innocent, for the 'guilt' of relatives is the extreme of injustice. It is both a violation of the blameless children's rights and hurts their normal growth.

At birth, every baby becomes a citizen in its own right and deserves the rights and respect enjoyed by other citizens, regardless of age. The state must ensure the safety and protection of every toddler. Unfortunately, whenever a mother is alleged to have committed a transgression, she will be jailed with her newborn if she has one, and the little one can only survive prison if the mother is set free.

Here, the child is treated not as a person but as part of a guilty mother, and is thus carried to jail like any other basic property that can be clutched along. Prison does not serve any of the child's best interests; by punishing the mother, it also endangers the welfare of an innocent baby.

Apparently, all our laws are silent on the continued detention of innocent, voiceless children. There is need to review our laws so that justice, other than injustice, is administered through them. Parliament should legislate against this unfair practice and the executive should take immediate steps to correct and suspend this lawful injustice!

We cannot continue to slumber when innocent individuals are spending the most crucial part of their lives in incarceration without any foreseeable compensation. Perhaps the children kept in prison should be enumerated and registered so that when they grow up, they are told the damage and injustice occasioned to them earlier, so they could seek redress.

Even the Bible condemns the punishing of children for their parents' transgressions; the proverbial eating of sour grapes by parents, only to endanger their children's dentition. *Ezekiel 18:2-13* partly says, "Parents have eaten sour grapes, thus their children's teeth are on edge ... there shall no longer be anyone among you who will repeat this proverb ... a son who is a thief, murderer, ... his death shall be his own fault."

Personal responsibility is fundamental. We cannot be liable for the misdeeds of our parents or relatives. Moreover whereas a mother and child are simultaneously imprisoned for a crime committed by one, the sentence can never be reduced on the understanding that it has been shared.

Such human rights abuse should not be ignored any longer. The legislature was not quite thorough when it passed the Children Act

(2003) and ignored to mention anything about this unfortunate oppression. The constituent assembly must have foreseen loopholes in the law and provided for such mechanisms as the Human Rights Commission, to consider all rights abuses and seek redress from government and pertinent agencies.

The commission is therefore challenged to look into this form of abuse. The 1995 constitution (article 50) mandates any Ugandan who believes the rights of any individual are infringed to raise the matter up with the constitutional court. The civil society could thus lead the way.

The law attaches criminal responsibility to the individual person and not to the community, unlike in traditional Africa when an offence was punishable to every member of the family. It is therefore necessary that innocent jailed children get compensated by government for the torture, trauma and all other sorts of suffering they have to endure.

By Venansio Ahahwe, published in The Weekly Observer, Kampala 19th April 2007

7. Government should tax weddings, anniversaries and love affairs

During the week ended, governments in East Africa announced national budgets to usher in a new fiscal year 2010/2011. Finance ministers Uhuru Kenyatta of Kenya, Clotilde Nizigama of Burundi, Syda Bbumba of Uganda, John Rwangombwa of Rwanda, and Mustafa Mkullo of Tanzania all promised a year of abundance for the common man. Poverty, hunger, disease and other social shortfalls will become a tale of times gone by – oh what a world!

The Comrade believes that national budget days are mere political rituals with trivial benefits for ordinary citizens. The purpose of a national budget is to honestly assess a nation's available resources and needs and thus determine priorities and sacrifices to make to derive utmost benefits, even with measly resources. Our budgets are drawn with political considerations, often aimed at giving the public false hopes. When do people ever recall the previous year's budget so as to ask their government to account? Never!

Well, this may not be our business. If you ask, The Comrade would suggest a tax regime on some humdrum projects that involve a lot of cash transactions but little, if any, sacrifice on the part of the recipients. Think of a wedding ceremony. It has become a culture for couples to fleece relatives, friends, workmates, and other acquaintances simply because they want to get married. They will arrange a luxurious fiesta, far beyond their capacity to sponsor, and transfer the burden onto others.

You must delay payment for your child's school dues, treatment for your mother, and edifice for your private home to contribute funds for an extravagant wedding. How this contributes to the national economy is a question. It is different from a man or woman who gets a bank loan to start a business. Government does not encourage public contributions to such a person's effort at all. It cannot ignore them so that businesses generate personal and national monies without difficulty. Rather, it will levy taxes as though to discourage business initiatives.

All the finance ministers should get red cards for such miscalculations. Let them tax wedding donations and gifts which couples amass without investing. Every couple that plans a luxurious wedding costing not less than a million shillings should also remit a percentage of their total budget to the government so that more and more people in a poor country should think of investment not lavishness. Plush weddings are a means of displaying personal wealth. Slack paupers and beggars have no business in this. In spite of all the pomp that attends to weddings nowadays, the rate of divorce and separation increases day-by-day. At their wedding, many couples are excited more about the public elation they will enjoy than about the commitment they would assume.

Yet, business people tend to appreciate personal responsibilities and required sacrifices they would make for their businesses to succeed. No wonder that people rarely reject their businesses like men and women do their spouses. The Comrade believes that partners cheat on each other and marriages crumble because couples have little to lose in monetary terms since all they invested were mere feelings and emotions. Taxation could help intending couples take matrimony more seriously.

Other than being a way to contribute to national development, taxation should be used to discourage unproductive ventures that waste people's resources, but are either expensive or harmful to personal and communal wellbeing. For instance, to discourage production or consumption of undesirable items such as polythene bags, high taxes are levied. To encourage consumption or utilisation of others such as computers and related accessories, taxes are reduced or waived.

It would make economic sense further for finance ministers to encourage individuals and families to make choices that promote their private welfare which feeds into national progress. Poor and uneducated people produce many children for example, and contribute highly to national poverty and illiteracy. To promote the adoption of manageable families, government can impose a tariff per extra pregnancy after a couple's third child.

By Venansio Ahabwe, published in Guardian on Sunday, Dar es Salaam 13th June 2010

8. Testing for HIV is not a cup of tea

How many of us would be comfortable to know for sure that the car by which we have chosen to make a memorable trip is destined for a fatal accident? Truth is, HIV and a shy population are a lethal combination, but the fear of reality is the absolute master of humanity. As long as we inhabit planet earth, it is foolhardy to assume that people could come to terms with any prospect of imminent personal death. Worry will always be etched on every individual face when death is mentioned.

Our ancestors, including Adam and Early man, spent honourable lives; long lives indeed. But their ultimate end was to lie lifeless in the ground and decompose long before their contemporaries could forget them. Every person knows with absolute certainty that come rain or shine, they will face death, having known both friends and foes succumb to it with utter docility and characteristic pain. Yet it remains horrifying to acknowledge that it is such 'a necessary end', as Shakespeare calls it, to which all are destined. For this reason, many people are religious, since religion teaches that to die is not to perish but to proceed to another phase of life.

It is thus understandable that the Minister of health Ms. Ana Abdullah has strongly challenged leaders to lead the way in taking HIV testing, and set a good precedent for other members of the public to emulate. While launching the third phase of Angaza Voluntary Counselling and Testing (VCT) services in Tanzania, on 10th May 2005, the Minister lambasted leaders who do not lead by example.

"If leaders came out and had these tests, the public would follow in their footsteps," she argued, with the conviction of a prophet.

She also claimed that male chauvinism is the fuel with which the Aids fire has been kindled. *Raisi mstafu* Ali Hassan Mwinyi supported the *waziri*, noting that knowledge of one's health status is paramount in forestalling the spate of the ravenous pandemic.

"It is better to tackle a problem from a position of knowledge," he observed with equal force. ('Take HIV tests, leaders urged', *The Citizen*, 11ᵗʰ May 2005).

The inevitable truth is that while Aids remains worrisome and ought to be confronted with bold confidence, the majority have got only half a mind to take a challenging step. Whereas it helps for everyone to know their status, very many people wish the secrets of their lives could remain guarded even against themselves.

Peering Eye believes that in the war against Aids, public screening will become a watchtower because knowing one's status is good for personal and general planning. It imposes a requirement for self-discipline after confirming that one is infected with the virus that causes Aids, which in turn demands a spirit of honesty, compassion for and from others, and avoidance of hazardous undertakings. This underscores accountability for one's own life, family, society and the nation, in preparation for the ultimate destination.

Aids screening is helpful for obtaining and accessing support for those who require and deserve it. The magnitude of the Aids epidemic must be known if appropriate interventions are to be designed and implemented, so long as those in authority accept that it is their duty to edify the sufferers. The facts about the disease cannot be obtained from mere speculation but by people freeing themselves from timidity, which puts nobody to any advantage but to increased health risks. Concrete facts are required to render the necessary support, and explore sufficient preventive measures for potential victims.

However, it is important to look at another facet of the problem. In addressing issues that involve human beings, it is important to understand that we are not dealing with angels. The minister lambasted leaders, but being a leader is no shield from natural human frailties, especially fear – the fear of lying helplessly in the claws of the ogre never to turn back. It takes extraordinary courage to accept that your days are numbered; especially in the absence of concrete mitigation programmes to take the edge off people's worries.

In pursuing to know the HIV status of individuals, we must watch the myriad of dire consequences that come with people knowing that they are infected with the virus. Families have broken because of Aids. Individuals who cannot cope with the prospect of dying soon are known to have committed suicide or lost interest in self-promotion work. Ostracism and rejection by the victim's companions have been reported in some circles. Loss of jobs can result as some employers lose faith in the suitability of certain individuals to perform particular tasks. When all is said and done, therefore, Hon. Abdullah is not inviting us to a tea party.

By Venansio Ahahwe, published in Sunday Citizen, Dar es Salaam, 29th May, 2005

9. Allow security guards to operate on patients too

The best news recently reported in The Citizen is that one does not have to seek a qualified medical worker in order to be treated at a health centre in this country. Professional health workers are so rare that security guards and other casual labourers are stepping in to save the situation. They can examine patients, operate scanning machines, perform laboratory tests, recommend hospital admissions, prescribe medication and administer injections in rural, official health centres. What is not clear is whether the same security guards have had chance to access the theatre and perform surgical operations on their clients. Who would then need a doctor?

Monduli and Longido districts have experienced unending shortage of trained medical practitioners and the authorities have not allowed the crisis to escalate. According to Ms. Mackrine Shao-Rumanyika, security guards and office attendants in that area have assumed roles of professional health workers and are treating patients in dispensaries and health centres ('Guards treating patients in Longido', *The Citizen* 27th March 2008).

The revelation is quite delightful. Mackrine is the coordinator of the Arusha-based NGO: Health Integrated Multisectoral Services (HIMS). During the White Ribbon Day at Lepurko Village, she disclosed that there was critical shortage of medical staff in the two districts, inhabited by nomadic pastoralists and that maternal and child mortality in that area soared unchecked.

Let it be known nonetheless that professional medical practitioners per se cannot stop death. They can actually accelerate it. Peering Eye wishes to adduce evidence that is already a public secret. The deadly surgical operations that were performed at Muhimbili hospital on Emmanuel Didas and Emmanuel Mgaya were not conducted by security guards or office attendants. Rather, it was by the 'best' medics to be found at the supreme referral hospital in Bongo.

Emmanuel Mgaya had developed acute headaches while studying for his final secondary school exams and was referred to Muhimbili Hospital for a brain operation to remove a suspected tumour that always caused migraine. When time came, the surgeon instead slit his athletic knee. Emmanuel Didas had his healthy skull opened to remove a brain tumour whereas he had been admitted for a knee operation after a motorbike accident. The former has since been condemned to a wheelchair, while the latter actually died. Amidst the scandal, security guards were clearly absent – and such deadly messes have not been reported in Monduli and Longido.

We can forgive a security guard who blunders in the course of performing a medical procedure. It is not his work, after all. If he advised a patient to drink injection fluid, you would still praise his level of concern. Someone, once upon a time, buried a needle into an injury on a patient's leg, seeing no need to open a fresh wound with syringe at the victim's buttocks. He still did better than the aforesaid experts who mutilated their clients' healthy organs. A security guard has no opportunity to inflict such damage, and an office attendant would have picked the actual file to make a mistake on the right organ.

Peering Eye thus congratulates the security guards of Longido and Monduli on their eccentric courage. They are real wa-Bongo. If they did not treat patients, who would? Government might not be aware that these communities exist or that they ever fall sick and require conventional medicine. Perhaps government mandate here is simply to set up buildings and deploy security guards to protect them from God-knows-what. The patients that turn up at these places are possibly stubborn trespassers and the treatment they get is the punishment the guards must give to discourage more visitors. The victims, however, discover that this is better than nothing.

The weapons which security guards hold to protect the dispensary premises are not syringes and stethoscopes. They are arrows, spears, and machetes. If they discover that the patients refuse to go away without services, they have added to their kit needles and infusions. To reduce endless rows at a health facility, it is good to deploy security guards – not doctors and nurses!

By Venansio Ahabwe, published in Sunday Citizen, Dar es Salaam, 13th April 2008

10. Highly earning, non-taxable jobs in town

Someone was doing his business but used my ignorance to earn profits. He made me hire a car for three hours on the understanding that he would show me a house to rent in the plush suburbs of the city whereas he had several personal places and people to visit.

At every stop, he would advise, "Please wait here as I talk to the landlady, the landlord etc" before we would move on miles away again.

In the end I paid him a huge allowance for messing up my day. Tanzania Revenue Authority should enlist a tax assessment consultant to identify all taxable businesses and ensure that they are indiscriminately taxed without fear or favour. I propose that Peering Eye takes the job because we have today noticed that highly lucrative businesses are ignored for taxation whereas wretched ones such biscuits hawkers and traders in makeshift squalid shops are taxed to the marrow.

Many such unfortunate traders have been forced to return to their villages. Yet the tax system is expected to be fair enough to encourage business enterprise and comprehensive to cover all business categories.

One business that has effectively evaded all taxation is the *dalali* enterprises. These are brokers for residential houses who are stationed all over the city, conducting risk-free business. They are everywhere if you want them, with their official business premises by the roadsides – on verandas or in tree-shades.

Their signposts inexpertly written – often shabbily scribbled as if by preschool infants trying out their undeveloped writing skills – are printed on trees, planks, or pieces of iron sheets and hung wherever the *dalali* spend their days. There need not be a house for the business premises, as that would mean paying rent and affecting the profits.

The estate agents usually sit drinking coffee, smoking, playing chess, gossiping, and listening to music from a nearby shop/pub or pushcart cassette seller. Some are often times seen sitting in the scorching sun all day long, donning sleeveless tee shirts.

Their only business investment is a mobile phone. To contact the *dalali*, you may find out from the classified free-of-charge announcements in the newspapers where they post their telephone numbers, which may be repeated for both existing and non-existing houses available for renting. Yet they do not need to buy the newspaper much as they may not have to be literate or able to speak English.

To be shown a single house, you must pay a minimum of shs5000/=. A *dalali* will take you to any house even though he knows it has been rented already. In the scotching Dar sun, the *dalali* might make you walk for miles, knocking at doors of several gates, to hear the house was occupied last week, yesterday, this morning, an hour ago, anything! Then, he might require that you hire a taxi to ride all over the city to a house in a sorry state – again you pay him for showing it to you.

If you finally come across an acceptable house and decide to take it, the *dalali* requires an allowance equivalent of one month rent from you i.e. you pay for thirteen months if you rent it for a year. The house owner must too part with a commission, which I cannot gauge, not being a landlord. It must be a good amount though, given the brokers' negotiation skills. In a good week, the *dalali* may bag two million shillings; non-taxable income.

When you occupy the house, the good *dalali* will keep in touch with you by visiting or telephone, especially when he is need of money. He will claim he wants to ascertain if you are comfortable with your accommodation. The interaction will end with a request for help or to lend some money and this is normally granted, considering that you are dealing with one who knows all the corners of your residence.

Of course, there are risks involved. When looking for a house, the *dalali* knows and will tell you all the details of the house to the least detail, inside-out. They have unlimited access to all such houses, from room to room, to such a point that the privacy of the house is laid bare. Should anyone suspect you of possessing loot-able valuables, it could be pretty easy to lead the gang to any part of the house.

With all these advantages at his disposal, the *dalali* business should be assessed and taxed accordingly. Why not?

By Venansio Ababwe, published in Sunday Citizen, Dar es Salaam 14th November 2004

Part 2: WOMEN AND MEN

11. Why men can reduce unplanned pregnancies

The reason unplanned pregnancies are rampant is that men do not care! An American feminist, Barbara Eherenreich asserts that if men were equally at risk of pregnancy, knowing that their bellies might swell as if they were suffering from end-stage cirrhosis, pregnancy would be classified as a sexually transmitted disease and abortions would be no more controversial than emergency appendectomies. Another critic once said that if men got pregnant, maternity leave would last two years with full pay, all methods of birth control would be 100 percent effective, and babies would stay in the hospital until they are toilet trained.

To this argument, The Comrade adds that all abortions, maternal deaths, and children on the street or abandoned should be counted on men. Society should stop blaming such cases on women while in the due course allowing men to roam freely, making more women pregnant. When children are born 'fatherless', it is neither because their fathers have died, nor that women can conceive by artificial insemination. Rather, the men that caused the pregnancies did not stay around to fulfil their parental roles. The community then sneers at the single parent, generally a mother, for being so careless and immoral as to produce a child without a father.

Ebbinah Clora recently wrote a compelling piece about unplanned pregnancies and accompanying venereal diseases in women. (See: "Reasons behind unwanted pregnancies and STIs in women", *The Guardian* 24th, March 2010). The glaring crack in the story is that nothing was mentioned about men for the problems facing women as regards unwanted pregnancies and sexual diseases. Yet, for every pregnancy or sexually transmitted infection afflicting a woman, there is a man implicated.

A pregnancy is an exhibit that some man has wandered into a woman's territory, crashed on her, and left behind trails of mischief written on the victim's framework. Every illegitimate pregnancy can be directly linked to the man who caused it in the first place; the difference being that a woman becomes the visible carrier of a man's intrusive character – the sperm. The decision or accident from which a pregnancy arises is not solely a woman's effort; and no man should ever feign innocence when the woman he has had an affair with is blamed and accused for acquiring an undesirable pregnancy.

In fact, all attempts to prevent unplanned pregnancies should place men at the core of the intervention. Many times, a woman may intend to avoid an unintended pregnancy but since she needs a man as a man needs her, she may not possibly reach an autonomous decision. Moreover, if every man had the capacity to take good care of his woman and her pregnancy to ensure that his seed grows and hatches in a healthy environment, we would not be talking of unwanted pregnancies at all. Many men go out of the way to make their sexual partners round-bellied without consideration as to how the subsequent condition would be taken care of to bring forth a hale and hearty offspring.

Unfortunately, the work of avoiding pregnancy always rests on the woman's back. A man may promise to wear a condom or withdraw during sex but instead do the contrary, and the resulting pregnancy will be counted on the woman. At another level, family planning and population control activists should not just concentrate on urging the poor and illiterate to produce few or no children.

These people cannot understand or heed such messages. Instead, wealthy and educated people should lead by example by reducing or avoiding pregnancies altogether. Wealthy people should stop looking at their riches as a form of compulsion to have children who will inherit them; rather it should put their contribution to the general welfare of society and nation that can benefit any citizen in need.

The feeling that only the poor, who have no means of catering for their children adequately, should drastically suppress their chances of childbearing is absurd. The Comrade thinks that it does not matter if one is wealthy or poor. Whether born of poor or wealthy parents, all children will inhabit the same earth and survive on the same resources, even if at varying planes. It is the enlightened who should abandon childbearing to give chance to the ignorant who cannot see the sense.

Moreover, a growing population may not be a bad idea if to conform to the Malthusian logic. The Rev Thomas Robert Malthus observed that: producing many children establishes a competitive environment among siblings which in turn produces individuals with slightly greater chances of survival.The weaker offspring will stay in a condition of misery that inevitably keeps the entire human community on constant endeavour for better living conditions. If humanity never faced this situation, 'it is probable that man might never have emerged from the savage state'. If we cannot influence men and wealthy families to lead the way in avoiding pregnancies, we should shut up and allow nature to run its course.

By Venansio Ahabwe, published in The Guardian on Sunday, Dar es Salaam 28th March 2010

12. Men should celebrate more when polygamy is outlawed

In marriage, a man faces some degree of suffering but it is even worse in a polygamous marriage. A friend once said that marriage is the exact variance of happiness. The experience of one condition directly means the absence of the other, and hence 'you are either happy or married'.

The Comrade has never been close to entering a polygamous marriage and has no experience whatsoever to draw from to discredit it. Given the level of familial conflicts we come across in our society, however, one can imagine that a man in a polygamous relationship is one to pity. Many a man in monogamous marriages would find it strenuous to impress their wives with material, social and emotional considerations. How a man in a polygamous relationship manages to ration his love, cash, physic, and other nuts and bolts to make a happy, stable and durable marriage is quite a wonder.

In the normal course of things, men should be at the forefront of banning polygamy. It is them who bear the burden of fending for several women and raising too many children borne of competing co-wives. There are other feminine and masculine issues we tend to sweep under the carpet but which we know can wear a man out and shorten his lifespan. A man should therefore not wait to be restrained by the law from taking a second, third, and forth wife.

The government of the republic of Malawi has drafted a law to penalise any man who marries more than one wife. Patricia Kaliati, the Minister of Gender, Women and Children Development says that polygamy is being outlawed mainly for two reasons: to help stop the growing spread of HIV and AIDS in the country and to ensure that each woman enjoyed her husband's undivided love.

Hon Kaliati said that a polygamous husband as a rule will have among his wives a favourite; one who takes the biggest chunk of his attention, leaving all the others to jostle the over the tiny balance. In such a situation, abuse of women's rights occurs, and can only be eliminated by abolishing polygamy. Supporters of this law are mainly women rights activists who praise it as a positive step in an effort to reduce the rampant scale of gender based violence.

The new law stipulates that any man who marries an additional woman, well knowing that he has another wife will be liable to a jail sentence of five years without the option of a fine. However, men who already have more than three wives will be barred from marrying any other woman but will not be prosecuted for being polygamous since the law was not in place at the time when they entered the marriage contract.

At a religious ceremony in the capital Lilongwe, President Dr Bingu wa Mutharika, who recently wedded his sweetheart Callista Chimombo, asked, "How do you have more than one wife and be happy about it?"

This is a question *The Comrade* would have asked if he too had the platform. Yet there is one other question that no one has asked so far: why is it women that are intensely working to abolish polygamy and sponsoring drastic laws against it?

The answer is that all the laws target men. The Malawian law, for instance would incriminate a man who knowingly marries a woman on top of the one he committed himself to earlier. The same law is silent about a woman who knowingly enters a marriage contract with an already married man. At the same, if a woman abandons his husband and marries another man, that man will be accused of grabbing another man's woman and it is the man to be penalised.

Where is justice? Where is a woman's responsibility? When we talk of gender based violence, rarely do we address issues that affect men, and some laws simply perpetrate injustice against them. The Malawian law should send both men and additional wives to the gallows – though care should be taken not to send them to same jail.

By Venansio Ahabwe, published in Guardian on Sunday, Dar es Salaam, 2nd May 2010

13. Is polygamy evidence of man's great concern for woman?

Your columnist intended to turn the spot on Nigeria, following the death of that country's first university educated president, Umaru Yar'Adua. It is a serious cause of worry for a president to die in office because what has happened elsewhere is that the governance of a country is sometimes seen as a family affair where the next alternative is usually a member of the deceased family. In the recent past, the only president who died in office and was not succeeded by his offspring is Levy Mwanawasa of Zambia. The other two were shamelessly succeeded on the throne by their sons: the current president of Togo Faure Gnassingbe succeeded his father Gnassingbé Eyadéma, as did the present leader of Gabon Ali Bongo Ondimba at the death of his father Omar Bongo Ondimba.

The Comrade was captivated by the eulogy of Goodluck Jonathan, Nigeria's acting leader who was sworn-in as de-facto president on the day of his immediate predecessor's interment. Mr Goodluck said, "Nigeria has lost the jewel on its crown and even the heavens mourn with our nation tonight." It is true; the late Yar'Adua was a jewel in many senses. If in no other perspective, *The Comrade* honours him for not turning the presidency into a family affair, for even in death, his moral disposition has allowed his countrymen to stand head high. Many leaders on this continent failed and still fail to separate state from family affairs. Their children and spouses are the base on which government derives functioning and survival. It was not so for Yar'Adua – and May he rest in peace!

****

Let us return to our topic of last week. When *The Comrade* praised the move to ban polygamy and rallied men behind the women's stab, he was confronted with a plethora of statistics. One online reviewer pointed out that to ban polygamy is 'a step towards the right direction' although it should not be used to denigrate the splendour of marriage as whole and the 'happiness' it brings to couples. He sounded like George Orwell's piggish slogan of 'four legs good, two legs better'.

Another commentator brought rather incredible data. He cited the logic of the secretary general of the Muslim Association of Malawi who recently said that the prohibition of polygamy will spark off an increase in the rate of prostitution. He noted that available information shows that the number of women exceeds that of men by over six percent in any given society in Africa. If every man married only one wife, therefore, many women would remain unattended to and they would ultimately look for men in any way possible, including through risky, immoral and deadly means.

The bloke went further to say that every polygamist, wherever you find him, is a reflection of what the name 'man' stands for: a Good Samaritan and an embodiment of authenticity. He advanced the craziest view that categorised some men as mere counterfeits. He argued that to say that 'some men are more equal than others' is to acknowledge the existence of two classes of men: real men and counterfeits. Thus, monogamous men often pass off as genuine products whereas they are mere imitations of the genuine species that the creator originally intended. Counterfeits tend to be cheaper and widespread whereas good quality, authentic products are always rare, costly and hard to discern. It is such rare men that can become polygamists.

As Good Samaritans, he went on, polygamists are guided by the concept of 'pro-social motivations'. It rejects the popular view that human behaviour is principally governed by 'self-interest'. Polygamists are not self-seekers. Rather, polygamy runs on the more complex view of both individual behaviour and social organisation that stress the virtues of duty, love and kindness. To marry a woman that would otherwise remain husbandless is an act of generosity and concern for others. Such thinking, *The Comrade* believes, is shaped by naivety if not just a malevolent way of shedding crocodile tears.

By Venansio Ahabwe, published in Guardian on Sunday, Dar es Salaam, 9th May 2010

14. To hang a man for being so much in love with women!

There are many young men on the street shopping for women's love and eventual marriage; but equally are women on the shelf yearning for reliable men as husbands. When a lovely chap shows up, however, he may be already married to another woman, yet willing to accommodate one or more lovers in a state of polygamy.

What does a young lady do in that case? Invade the colony to grab a chunk of another woman's territory or wait until an unclaimed guy appears, God-knows-when? Who is to blame if an impatient woman chooses to raid a sovereign zone? It cannot be the man who is being competed for, but the lady who marches into an already occupied territory.

A human rights organisation, known as Mifumi, has petitioned the constitutional court in Uganda to declare polygamy illegal because it violates the right to equality between man and woman. The petitioners believe that a man who marries two or more women is ultimately telling the world that he is too important to be satisfied with a lone woman's love. This kind of egotism is deplorable and the women are praying that court should declare it criminal.

This is not a woman's war though. It should be a man's war as well. If every man was to marry two wives, there would not be enough women for all men since the global population of women and men narrowly matches. The problem therefore is not merely that women in polygamous marriages are abused at all, but that the practice of polygamy is both selfish and a recipe for disaster. Men who are deprived of love and marriage opportunities can easily resort to violence and bring about social mayhem.

Moreover, a woman who accepts to become an additional wife is obliquely telling the world that some men are superior to others. One is tempted to believe that indeed a man who becomes polygamous is a super man. Many men - *The Comrade* is one of them - struggle day and night to impress a single woman. That some men can simply meet the basic needs of numerous women is indeed inscrutable!

The Comrade recalls the 1990s at college where it was free-grazing. Some bachelors were so popular with girls that they had the luxury of flirting with one after another as other bachelors watched with envy. Many girls cared less if they got only a fraction a lad's attention. A girl too would be very competitive but boys strove for her undivided attention; quitting at once if she seemed to ration her love. Both men and women have the freedom to claim full attention or just a portion of it.

Interestingly, anti-polygamy crusaders are inadvertently sending out a message that equality among women and men is a far cry. Where the principle of agreement between two consenting adults rules, activists seem to say that a woman cannot make a correct and conscious decision, and thus needs a law for protection. This is quite an insult to women. *The Comrade* is a Christian and does not support polygamy. He thinks, nonetheless, that many women take up polygamous marriages wilfully, and are responsible for the consequent events.

Many of the interventions geared at promoting women's rights often undermine the intended beneficiaries' abilities to effectively stand up against tendencies that keep them down. The best solution, for instance, should be capacity building for young women to appreciate the social, physical, and economic implications of polygamous marriages; and why and how such marriages should be avoided. No man will marry a woman at gunpoint.

Marriage is a free choice and forced marriages inherently flawed. That there may soon be a law to punish men for violating women's rights by marrying many of them is ridiculous, crazy and absurd. Prominent polygamists like Jacob Zuma could have to defend themselves at the ICC. You may not be Jacob Zuma but, in future, it may be illegal for your son or daughter to marry from a preferred tribe, religion, class, or family.

By Venansio Ahabwe, published in Guardian on Sunday, Dar es Salaam 21st February 2010

15. To hell with male prostitutes!

A reader of *Sunday Citizen* requesting anonymity has sent me email which I do hereby quote verbatim in part. "The presence of prostitutes on our city streets is yet another manifestation of men's superiority over women, a case of male chauvinism and insularity which indeed is abhorrent! It is a shame that as a man, you are able to narrate how absurd the situation of prostitutes has become when it is you men who are sustaining them on streets and praying hard that their predicament may increase so that you continue to have fun from their misery.

She went on, "Don't you know that women have the same feelings as you? Why then do you believe that only male tourists, travellers and city dwellers are entitled to sex? What happens to the women travellers, tourists and thousands of unmarried women? As long as decision makers – all of them men – are glossing over the presence of prostitutes, there will never be equality. Let there be male prostitutes as well!"

Ladies and gentlemen, we are in shit! I have never loathed progressive thinking, creativity and modernity. I neither ever harboured a negative thought against gender equity and the need for equal opportunities of men and women alike. That is, in all spheres of life. What has never crossed my mind is the idea of a male prostitute.

To my utter shock, I have now been asked to participate in this debate. Male what? God in heaven! What have we come to? Let it be known that if such a thing were to be in Bongoland, I would oppose it with all my might. Let it be erased totally from someone's psyche because it might cause us problems. I do not have the required clout to campaign to join the next parliament or city council in order to move a motion outlawing all forms prostitution and calling for the burning of any dictionary that contains such a word. Of course it is too late to contest for presidency, but my advice to those who are in time to do so is, promise to ban prostitution immediately.

I would not hesitate to adopt the Iraqi insurgents' method: wrap myself in some chemical and explode right in the middle of such an accursed group of desperate men, should they appear on the streets as prostitutes. Apart from prostitution being immoral, it is unacceptable that some man should expose us to such a level of insult and indignity merely for the sake of money. That is one reason I am annoyed with the Anglican Communion for ordaining a bishop who admits playing female marital roles in bed.

Prostitution is shameful. Whereas ladies have often paraded themselves on the streets for men to access, no man is known to have possibly come up openly to accept that he chases after prostitutes. Those who support the prostitutes' continued stay on the streets say that they do so in the interests of other people who may require their services, not themselves.

What is clear however is that it is the men who buy prostitutes. Again it is foolhardy to imagine that those attractive women, codenamed prostitutes, are not getting enough customers. If customers were rare or nonexistent, the girls would abandon the streets. It should be remembered the men who buy prostitutes do so under the cover of darkness at night. All of us know them, and we have seen them, haven't we? Let me remind you if you still doubt that you know any. Stop reading; look at the man before you. He is the man I am talking about.

It is better for the women who lack men to suffer than breaking the few remaining families merely to give women similar opportunities to be immoral as men. Moreover, nobody has ever seen grass moving from the field to look for a goat; it is the goat that goes to the field in search of grass.

By Venansio Ahabwe, published in Sunday Citizen, Dar es Salaam, 8th May 2005

16. Surrender public transport to women!

Peering Eye has a mind to defect from Adam's community and join daughters of Eve. He is tired of the way men continue to edge the female species to the sidelines of public transport, when everyone knows that women are more careful whenever they are behind the wheel. Much as we have seen men invade women's typing gizmos to work as office secretaries, we have not yet witnessed a proportionate number of women working as drivers or conductors in the public transport industry.

After a careful consideration of the behaviour of the two categories of humankind on the road, I have come to a conclusion that one is safer travelling in a car at whose helm is a lady. The number of reckless female drivers is so insignificant; those known to have caused accidents are simply unnoticeable. Again, women are generally well disciplined in public; they prefer to defer their other side till they are in the private quarters of their homes. And this is as important as it is necessary for us the road users, for we would be spared the outrage of the male species who carry their grudges beyond their bedrooms and living rooms into buses and cabs. Little wonder that our roads are awash with accidents daily.

Now hear this. It is an accident to find a lady-driver involved in a serious, deadly accident. They normally cause minor road mishaps. It is actually difficult, even impossible, to find an accident in which two women drivers are altogether involved. It is often a man that must ram into a woman driver's car and will naturally blame her merely for being a woman.

A woman behind the wheel is a gracious, comforting spectacle. To drive a car behind a woman's is to experience the gentleness that God might have preferred us to exhibit whenever we are executing business on the road. No woman driver will ram into your car from behind. She will naturally keep a safe distance, though she might be in a hurry to get to her destination. A woman does not drive off the road to inconvenience other travellers – pedestrians, wheelbarrow pushers, or cyclists.

It is a blessing for a pedestrian to cross the road when a lady-driver is approaching. She will not knock you down; she cannot shed innocent blood. Women tend to seriously observe traffic rules and are calculative when overtaking. They are not so rude, opportunistic or selfish road users as men.

Precisely, I am complaining against the near total absence; the virtual exclusion of women from the public transport sector. We do not have female daladala or taxi drivers. There are no female conductors simply to open for and collect the fares from the passengers.

In government, all vehicles are entirely in the hands of men, and so are those of the very many nongovernmental agencies. Even women's organisations that claim to champion the women's cause often exclusively recruit men as drivers to do the salaried work. Not even the Ministry responsible for women's welfare and emancipation employs a female driver.

Yes, women ought to be blamed for never taking serious interest in the field of driving. The few who venture into a driving school have acquired a personal or family car. They do not learn driving as a way of earning a living, just like men do; yet they too have lives and families to sustain and are actually more disadvantaged. It is clear that women are not willing to talk about their own thoughts, and have done little to boost their economic stature by participating in commercial driving and the general transport industry.

Thus, deliberate effort should be made to bring the ladies on board, as they would make the public transport industry both safer and enjoyable. Bringing women into this sector would be a monumental feat of earthmoving.

Such a development would bring sanity and good order to the field, eliminate traffic jams, and save travellers from regular, urgent deaths and injuries. Unfortunately, women prefer to keep their noses clean, they might not accept such a seemingly risky proposition, beneficial as it may be.

By Venansio Ahabwe, published in Sunday Citizen, Dar es Salaam, 13th February 2005

17. Join your lady in a labour-ward

Women who undertake childbirths tell of indescribable levels of pain they experience inside the labour ward, while delivering a child. Some say that the moment of labour amounts to a near-death incident! Women who have gone through it have principally boasted of their supreme endurance, but a man can today witness the tale of agony felt by their wives by escorting the women into the delivery room.

When I used to stay at home, women in my village would (and perhaps still do) gather around a woman in labour, supporting her to bring forth a new baby. They would chase away any peeping man, even her husband! Until she had been fully calmed and cleaned, along with her baby, no man whatsoever would be allowed to come close to congratulate her.

Subsequently, husbands found an excuse to run up and down pursuing nothing in particular, if only to show that they too were labouring to support the childbirth. Nowadays, townsfolk prefer to stand outside the ward, occasionally jumping into the car and driving away, to return shortly with say, a congratulation card – since they are basically barred from the labour ward.

As a rule, the child's father has to wait to be told of his wife's experience at delivery. He learns second-hand what child has been born. A midwife emerges from the room to declare, "It is a baby-girl or baby-boy", before the husband dispatches numerous phone texts to friends and relatives, announcing the glad news.

This is very unfair. It is cowardly of men to run away whenever literal childbearing is mentioned. Husbands should be more proactive. Some fathers-to-be have been cited waiting at a nearby bar when their women are inside the labour-ward. This is absurd for, at some point, the delivering mother would be in a coma and unable to know what is happening around her. The child might even be stolen.

A father should essentially see it as a duty to be inside the delivery room at the time of a child's birth, to witness the golden moment. It should be your right to see your own child being born. To watch firsthand the entire chapter, to personally cut the cord, to hold your child before anyone else! What a memorable experience it should be!

In the western world, some parents consider it a great misfortune for a man to miss such a great event, which enables you to tell your children in future about the first moments when you held them and how emotional it was.

In England as in America, it would be deemed brutal for a man not to be by his wife's bedside to care and share the labour pains. According to Britain's National Childbirth Trust, partners accompany more than ninety percent (90%) of the women giving birth. In some cases, about a dozen people, close friends and family members, would turn up. The line-up of relations and supportive friends wanting to be in the delivery room is thus increasingly becoming an issue of great concern, as it has given rise to "labour room parties" which in turn inconvenience the medical staff.

It has been proposed that being at the birth is a good thing: it sets a pattern for fathers to remain involved through children's lives. It helps them to appreciate the beauty of childbirth and prepares a man to cooperate fairly with his partner in looking after children. It generates a sense of emotional attachment. It also helps the couple to discuss, from a shared perspective, the need for family planning.

It is fulfilling to have a baby and also an opportunity to be the first to counsel your wife through her difficult time of labour! Absence of husbands from the ward leaves many men unaware that the wife was in a life or death situation. Experts warn that men need to be counselled about the sights and sounds to expect during labour as some men would collapse, watching their women going through intense pain. Would you collapse?

By Venansio Ahabwe, published in Sunday Citizen, Dar es Salaam, 12th March, 2006

18. Women often inflict violence on men

When a woman calls a man a chimpanzee, she is not asking him to be kind. She is telling him to be wild. She therefore becomes the initiator of violence. Yet when you start a fire, it will burn in any direction, even towards you!

To purge marriages and families of regular violence, it is important to consider the various dimensions of cruelty that, in many cases, are the hallmarks of some homes. Ideally, men and women should live in mutual love and support as role models for their children in their care.

Last Monday, the Young Women's Christian Association (YWCA) celebrated the 'Week Without Violence' in Dar es Salaam where the Prime Minister's wife, Regina Lowassa presided. She advised women to break the shackles of silence in the face of fierce acts meted on 'women, children and vulnerable groups' ('Speak out against violence – Regina', *The Citizen* 17th October 2007).

Peering Eye however contends that violence afflicts men and women in nearly the same measure. Of late, there has been growing concern that the media, in reporting the subject of violence, has adapted an 'anti-male approach', portraying men in total negative light.

Men too have rights to protect. For instance, when analysing suicide, it is not seen as a problem that primarily afflicts men but generally as a social problem. Women seldom commit suicide. The argument on violence is often subjective as pundits tend to depict men as stony fiends with infinite propensity to cause harm.

Violence is caused by many factors, which cannot be squarely attributed to men, and these factors may be overt or hidden. The cause-effect of violence must be appreciated. Sometimes men resort to violence as a response to the concealed cruelty occasioned on them by their female partners in the quiet of their house. Violence takes many forms, including emotional, physical, psychological, or sexual.

A woman may insult her man, belittle him, deny him food or sex, accuse him of extravagance or infidelity, or humiliate him before their children or guests. In the circumstances, the female partner is not merely provoking the man to violence, she is largely subjecting him to violence. In evaluating the scope and magnitude of violence in relationships, homes and communities, we must widen our mentality beyond the physical perspectives such as rape, beating, injury or death.

The scope of violence must be broadened to include behaviour that provokes hostility. A partner may deliberately adopt mannerisms intended to embarrass or humiliate another. S/he may remind the other of an ugly past, swear to teach the other a lesson, call them funny names, or point out a partner's poor sexual performance. All these are acts of violence and must be addressed.

A woman must not cause such situations, simply believing that we shall sympathise if she suffers – and nor should a man! Many women do, often unaware that they are contributing to the escalation of violence in society.

Unfortunately, it is only when a person appears weeping, physically hurt, bruised or killed that we conclude that violence has occurred. As shown above, much of the rampant brutality among men and women takes the form of 'tolerable' acts, which must be addressed if we are to reduce, even eliminate violence in society.

It has been suggested that violence is meted out as an answer to the shame a person has experienced. Unfair as it is, some scholars have referred to violence as "a source of pride and a defence of honour". This means a person who feels that his dignity has been wounded would tend to reclaim it in many ways, violence inclusive. It has been argued, in fact, that humans are inherently violent; the president, the bishop, the typist, the bank teller, the street sweeper, and the journalist are all potentially violent if they were not to exercise self-restraint.

By Venansio Ahabwe, published in Sunday Citizen, Dar es Salaam, 21st October 2007

---

19. Cheating in marriage? You cheat yourself.

A lustful man breaks the matrimonial vows; he begets a baby girl with a secret mistress and hides the news from his official wife. He is able to support the concubine and her daughter through adolescence and school, to attain a marriageable stature. She grows to become beautiful and admirable; then his own son – born of his wedded wife – identifies her for a future wife and proposes marriage. She is introduced to the family and the boy's mother gets over the moon about the quality of woman her son is bringing to the family.

The father, on the other hand, is shocked to learn that a marriage between a brother and sister is imminent. The status of his children will soon be a muddle: his son will partly become his son-in-law while his daughter will also double as a daughter-in-law. How would he manage such a relationship? He is understandably troubled at the tragic trend of events; he decides to face the reality and block the impending marriage of siblings who are unknown to each other.

The man calls his son aside and tells him the truth, "My son! Now that you are planning to start a family, you are no longer a child but a man like me. I am proud of you, thus I must share with you what it means to be a man. It is quite a challenge. I have been married to your mother all this time but ... eeer ... Satan tempted me somehow and I s**ed another woman; she conceived and gave birth to a girl. I have never introduced my bastardly clutter to the family ... eeer ... now; you are planning to marry her. The girl you are courting for marriage is my daughter. You cannot marry your sister. It is an abomination!"

This revelation hits the young man like a thunderbolt. He cannot see how to withdraw his affection for his lover and abandon her at the last hour. He thought their love for each other was irretrievable as they have sworn into each other's ears, eyes, armpits, mouths, breasts, and heart that they would marry, even at the point of death. His father offers to give up all property in his possession to the amorous son if he could look for another lover. After a long contemplation, the young man rejects his father's supplications and the case ends up in the woman's court.

Yet, the boy's mother has been charmed by the beauty and manners of her prospective daughter-in-law. She strongly believes that the only girl her son could marry is the one she has seen. For the first time, the father confesses his sin: narrates how he has had an extramarital affair that resulted in a girl child, whom the young man was dying to marry. Apologising to his connubial wife, he asks her to support his position against their children's marriage. She refuses.

"My dear," she starts, "thank you for the confession. You are henceforth forgiven. It was only human that you fell into such an error. Incidentally, your daughter's lover is not your son."

The man's eyes widen and he roars, "What? My son is not my child? She goes on, "He is not your son. Of all our four children, it is Michael whose father I am sure of. It is the shambaboy who was always available for me as you spent most of your time cutting deals with businessmen and women."

By Venansio Ahabwe, published in Sunday Citizen, Dar es Salaam 16th December 2007

20. Beautiful women wanted urgently

Tenders are invited from qualified and reputable individuals and companies for the supply of beautiful, young ladies on a daily contract basis. The services for tender are in the following categories and you can bid for one category or any combination of categories, indicating the delivery period for each lot.

Category one: slender light skinned girls with considerable ambition and deep affinity for adventure. Category two: fleshy looking ladies of any complexion and height, with reasonable flexibility both in character and action, ready to take advantage of any available opportunity to excite clients.

All submissions will be evaluated based on the most competitive bid and the least delivery period. Interested suppliers for the above items may request further information and bidding documents from Peering Eye at a non-refundable fee of T.shs 1,000,000/= (one million shillings).

All bids must be submitted in sealed envelopes clearly marked "Tender for the supply of beautiful women" to reach Peering Eye not later than 17:00 hours each day before the end of this year. Tenders will be opened on the same day of submission, and bidders, their representatives or the very items of supply are free to attend the bid opening.

This advert has been prompted by a recent proliferation of beauty contests within and out of Dar es Salaam, as young ladies in each locality compete to outdo each other in terms of physical appearance as observed by a man's eye. It used to be Miss Tanzania but as time wore on, every hideout realised it was important to declare their beauty. There is currently a 'Miss somewhere' or 'Miss something'. Everywhere, beauty pageants are the order of the day; with young women engrossed in cutthroat competition to excel at public exhibitions for their personal qualities, features, and other endowments to be judged.

The scantly dressed young girls parading their near-nakedness for public consumption are always exposing whole lengths of limbs up to heap-level, in all shapes and sizes of legs – bow-shaped, meaty, bony, scratched, and etcetera. Today, you might possibly hear of a Miss Ilala, Miss Mbezi, Miss Magomeni, Miss Tabata, Miss Kivukoni, Miss Mwenge, Miss Mikocheni, Miss Kigamboni, Miss Kariakoo, Miss Mwananyamala, Miss Ubungo, Miss Kimara, Miss University, Miss shule ya msingi, Miss Airport and so on and so forth.

Religious leaders will probably join the fray to prove that their congregations too are comprised of beautiful members. Available evidence shows that religious leaders would always want to keep in step with current trends by doing what their followers like, which will attract more people and money in the temple; the reason traditional church hymns have been abandoned for nightclub type of music since it appeals to the youth and the playful other than the prayerful. Before we know it therefore, we shall hear of Miss Assembly church, Miss St. Columbus, Miss Cathedral, Miss Miracle centre, Miss Holy prophet or Miss Gospel ministry, if to attract young people since music alone seems to be getting a little old-fashioned.

The beauty craze is really being pursued with hysterical abandon, so to be democratic, it is important to uphold the people's wishes and interests. This is a democratic nation, and democracy comes at a cost sometimes of the moral fabric of the society, such as making huge expenditures to be entertained to nude or semi-nude female humans and upholding strange standards to choose beauties. In a liberal economy like this, pageants are an economic activity sponsored by the most lucrative enterprises and also attracting many clients. It is for this reason that Peering Eye is proud to participate in nation building.

Ours will however involve the selection of soul models as well. We are spending so much time taking care of the outside appearance that the inner person will soon perish because of being completely neglected. We must be aware that whereas man sees the outside, God the highest judge sees the inside.

By Venansio Ahabwe, published in Sunday Citizen, Dar es Salaam 24th July 2005

Part 3: CULTURE, RELIGION AND SPIRITUALITY

21. Begging and almsgiving are morally wrong

You might find this story scandalous, sadistic, and altogether inhuman. It touches a sore part of our society, which we have come to accept and promote with gay abandon and casual generosity, to worsen the social, economic and moral hurdles confronting us.

I recently lost a substantial amount of money to beggars in Dar es Salaam. I had been attending Holy Mass at St. Peter's Parish Oysterbay. The presiding priest spoke strongly about the virtue of sharing and almsgiving. Focussing on the biblical story of a poor man, Lazarus, who is said to have been rewarded with heavenly glory, whereas his rich neighbour was incarcerated in hell, the priest made two statements that have since unsettled my social and economic outlook. He said that a person can easily tell how far or near they are to God: the distance you keep from the needy, is the same distance that exists between you and God. He added that what comes vertically from God to man must necessarily proceed horizontally from man to man.

Outside the church, several cripples had gathered to tax the worshippers. Truth be said, not all people with disabilities are beggars. Like all other humans, some people with disabilities are very active and productive society members. The ones I am talking about, however, had not turned up at church for the Sunday prayers. They were on a business mission, and I think they were smiling to themselves as the priest harangued the congregation, reminding us of the bitterness and anguish the rich man was subjected to because of his hapless neighbour, Lazarus.

When Mass ended, and as we left church, we dipped hands into our pockets and dished out cash, ostensibly to please God and keep near him. Christianity aside, almsgiving is one of the five pillars of Islam, and

41

it is highly revered and practised in Moslem life. Now assured of such generosity, beggars will always assemble near church or mosque, stand at road junctions, shop verandas, and hotel entrances. The blind, led by a child, will go around open pubs and bus stands, asking for alms. Some able-bodied persons too will feign disability if this may enable earn money.

I am yet to be schooled about the wisdom of a person dipping into their purse and ploughing out the spoils of their hard work, simply to share with the have-nots. Socially and economically, perhaps even spiritually, begging and almsgiving are very retrogressive. Begging itself can be so dangerous to society; it would promote indolence and the dependency syndrome. The person who relies on others' generosity is robbed of dignity and selfconfidence. As a consequence, they become passive in development matters, as they know and accept to be mere objects of charity.

At the same time, some genuinely disabled persons, especially those in wheelchairs and the blind require guides to go around begging. Usually, the guides happen to be children who either never enrol for school at all or are forced to drop out in order to provide the service. As a result, the guides are likely to learn begging as a way of life and therefore take up the habit later on. It is actually true that begging is fairly a good income generating activity. Many people, after realising that begging can easily be a way to access assistance, the reason indeed able-bodied individuals would fake disabilities to qualify for the alms. This is immoral and very wrong.

Almsgivers feel that they have a moral obligation to care for the helpless. Yet, almsgiving and begging are reciprocal; people beg because there are almsgivers out there, but again people give alms because there are beggars. If there were no almsgivers, there would be no beggars and vice-versa. This is not to say that it is unimportant to help the needy, but it should be done sensibly.

God should be the happier if the well-to-do gave fishing nets instead of fish to the needy. Potential and actual beggars need to be incorporated in the long-term development equation, not fed on handouts. They need to be mobilised and empowered, through say education, vocational skills, capital and saving schemes.

No amount of money given to a beggar can help them to abandon their trade. Begging is an art which when you perfect it will surely yield handsomely. Even if they earned heavily one day, beggars will not buy and wear clean clothes because they know that nobody will pity a well-dressed person. They prefer to dress in tatters. They will not bathe because they believe they must appear pathetic to be pitied. They cannot smile because they think that no one will feel sorry for a happy person. By giving alms, we support them remain in their condition forever.

By Venansio Ahabwe, published by Sunday Citizen, Dar es Salaam 27th March, 2005

22. Let's check virgins, Mama Kikwete!

Mama Salma Kikwete was delighted to see multitudes of virgins in Swaziland where she recently attended a Reed Dance. This is a ceremony that developed from the umcwasho custom where only childless, unmarried young girls would be placed in a female regiment, and if any of them fell pregnant before marriage, her family would pay a cow as fine to the local chief.

Thus, the Swazi young girls struggle to keep their virginity and to display it in an eight-week ceremony that climaxes into the Reed Dance. Elsewhere, in some cultures, virginity was so much treasured that girls who infringed rules regarding chastity might be ostracised.

Peering Eye believes nevertheless that there is no scarcity of virgins in this land really, so mama Kikwete does not have to look far away in Swaziland to admire virgins. Today's weddings habitually involve the women wearing milk-white wedding dresses, which by extension symbolise the bride's virginity, according to the Western cultures we copy.

Hopefully, all Bongo women who wear white at their wedding ceremonies are virgin. If truth be told moreover, virginity might not be a perfect custom, and is at times condemned. Critics say that very often, calls for abstinence are based on misleading or distorted information. The need to prevent Aids infections through abstinence has been jumbled with "moral renewal" for example, and the youth cannot tell which of the two is really critical.

Again, restrictions on sexual activity for extended periods of time might be emotionally or spiritually harmful. Sexual oppression might lead to various behaviour problems. Anthropologists and social historians have also noted that many cultures, which formally place a high value on abstinence, actually have a large amount of premarital sexual activity in which there is no actual sexual intercourse. Therefore it might not be surprising that cases of sodomy are on the increase, and probably so are masturbation, oral sex and etcetera.

Philosopher Bertrand Russel, in his book "Why I am not a Christian" argues that to avoid sexual relationship before marriage was naïve and unwise and that to do so would, in the long run, lead to far more unhappiness than if sexual activity was engaged in. With abstinence, a person restrains oneself from gaining pleasure, especially by suppressing their sexual appetite. One gives up some degree of sexual activity, namely sexual intercourse.

The value of abstinence is that it helps individuals to channel their sexual energies into other more 'acceptable' activities. Abstinence is also regarded as a form of spiritual discipline which "elevates" a person beyond the normal life of desire, by following a path of renunciation. It is often viewed as an admirable act of self-control; a display of one's strength of character to hold back a person's basic emotional wishes. It is considered an essential way to reach a particular intellectual or spiritual condition, religiously speaking.

Boys too need to uphold virginity because scientifically, sexual abstinence is said to confer numerous health benefits. Lack of abstinence on the part of male humans is said to cause a reduction of energy. Biologists suggest that loss of semen through ejaculation results in a depletion of vital nutrients such as lecithin and phosphorous which are also found at high levels in the brain.

Conversely, saving the semen allegedly allows it to be restored into the bloodstream to aid healthy body development. In fact, it was once believed that numerous mental and physical diseases in men were caused by loss of nutrients through seminal discharge – undermining a man's health, vitality and intellectual prowess.

In Swaziland as elsewhere, abstinence is the heart of virginity, which is closely interwoven with personal or family honour. Loss of virginity before marriage might be seen as a matter of deep shame. In many Bantu cultures, there were traditional practices which involved "virginity testing": a female elder would be deployed to do virginity inspection of young, unmarried girls. What of this mama Salma?

By Venansio Ahabwe, published in Sunday Citizen, Dar es Salaam, 10th September, 2006

23. Just how far should modern religion glorify violence?

A church group in America has explained that American soldiers are being killed in Iraq as vengeance from God. The Rev. Fred Phelps, founder of Westboro Baptist in Kansas, contends that a country (America), which harbours gays, is not worthy of defending, so God is punishing them because of the homosexual trends in their country. The church members have been demonstrating at soldiers' funerals across the nation, with messages such as "God hates fags" and "God hates you."

In another appalling episode, a rightwing American evangelist and religious broadcaster Pat Robertson (75) recently called on his mighty country to assassinate a President of a sovereign country, Venezuela's Hugo Chavez. Chavez is a regular critic of the US, thus Robertson's remarks came amid tense relations between the US and Venezuela. Robertson said, "We have the ability to take him out ... the time has come to exercise that ability ... we don't need another $200 billion war to get rid of one strong-arm dictator ... have some of the covert operatives do the job and then get it over with."

Ironically, the Pope had just urged Muslims to join Christians in trying to combat the spread of terrorism. Condemning what he called the "cruel fanaticism" of terrorism, Pope Benedict XVI while meeting the Moslem community in Germany underscored the Muslim leaders' responsibility to educate the younger generation in the ways of peace. He warned that the world risked exposure to "the darkness of a new barbarism", adding that terrorism endangers the lives of so many people and hinders progress toward world peace."

The spate of terrorism, which is wrecking global peace and stability besides souring international relations, is said to be deriving much of its fuel from Islamic fundamentalism. Most suicide bombers regard themselves as God's servants, suffering a martyrs' death by carrying out the will of God: to act on the behalf of God by striking at the enemy even if this brings death to the agent. He will die in body but live forever in God's glory!

From the foregoing, it is apparent that most religions have inherent terrorist tendencies; even in the way they instruct their members about the nature of God. They terrorise their followers by focusing more on the dangers that arise from ignoring God's ways than on the rewards associated with being in God's favour. They depict God as a harsh judge, very unhesitant to unleash catastrophe and destruction on people who fail by some degree to meet his demands? In which case believers would revere God, not out of pure conviction but fearing the possible repercussions of sinfulness. The commonest rhetoric in religious circles is to remind people of the possible mayhem awaiting them once they fail to uphold specific religious, if Godly, standards proclaimed by 'God's messengers'.

Modern-day evangelists have mustered the rude and abusive art of subduing listeners, you would think God favours the people who insult and despise others. Christian fundamentalists often slander against those who do not subscribe to their faith and consider it worthy to confront and overcome the wicked by any means as aforementioned. This perhaps explains why American evangelicals improved President George Bush's bid for Presidency, and continue to flirt with him despite the mess and mayhem as a result of the Iraq misadventure.

Many religious aficionados world-over have got an awful view of God as a merciless punisher who would unleash violence, humanly speaking, on people who "displease" Him. To displease God sometimes is seen as to worship in a different style perceived as evil by a person, unable to acknowledge his evil nature that makes him disrespect others.

Christian teachers are obsessed with self-praise and vilification of others who do not profess their faith. And this practice reverberates among young generations, for they are so impressionable as to espouse such idiosyncrasy, which undermines the spirit of respect for humanity and for others' beliefs. In many religions it is laudable to refer to members of other faiths as "wicked", "fools", "kafir" and etcetera.

Rather than the virtues of goodness and humility, young people are being encouraged to be bold and forceful in charging at people of other faiths, forgetting that this is irreligious if desirable. The current glorification of aggressive behaviour by both Christian and Islamic fanatics is perhaps the gravest misuse of holy responsibility. The Creator must be watching in open-mouthed shock!

By Venansio Ahabwe, published in Sunday Citizen, Dar es Salaam, 4th September 2005

24. The hilarious side of Jesus Christ's suffering

During the Easter period, many preachers tend to emphasise the fact that Jesus Christ suffered a great deal and faced a brutal death. In describing the torment that he underwent, some preachers express such fury as could fire their congregation into spontaneous street riots to lynch the Saviour's killers, if they met them. If today's Christians lived at the time of Jesus and witnessed the Way of the Cross, perhaps there would have been a possibility of genocide against the folks that tortured Jesus.

Yet, the entire chapter of the Saviour's suffering, as recorded in the Bible, was interspersed with numerous funny episodes that can make serious Christians both laugh and derive rich spiritual insights. There is no need for a Christian to shed tears for the suffering Jesus faced, which was principally for the serious benefit of sinners.

Jesus laughed at the people who blindly followed as a crowd bullied him. He turned to them and said, "... do not weep for me; weep instead for yourselves and for your children"" (Luke 23: 27-28). This group could educe laughter indeed as they did not know where their sympathies should have been placed. They behaved more like a proverbial politician who turned up at a schoolgirl's funeral. When he was given the chance eulogise, the politician said that 'the deceased was development-oriented man', to the amusement of mourners.

There is a young man who brought even more fun at the arrest of Jesus. He had apparently gone to bed early that day. Amidst the chaos, the boy simply picked a sheet of cloth and joined the torturous throng. Suddenly, the mob turned against him but as he fled, '...he left the cloth behind and ran off naked' (Mark 14: 51-52). What is amusing is not merely the nudity of the young man as he sped off; it also shows how poor judgement can be embarrassing.

Another element that arises is that we often carry other people's crosses. Jesus nearly died under the weight of his cross before he reached Calvary. Seeing this, the pesky mob forced an unsuspecting passer-by, Simon the Cyrenian to carry the bulky cross. The mob realised that Jesus needed relief but why none of them rendered the help is another matter. A rampaging mob can never be single-minded, so it is wise to take to your heels if you encounter them, in the absence of teargas.

Another comedy involved Simon Peter. This man claimed that he was the bravest, ready to defend Jesus to the point of death. "Lord, I am prepared to go to prison and to die with you," he assured his master (Luke 22:33). Indeed, he drew his sword and cut off one ear of the slave of the high priest during the arrest of Jesus. Soon after, however, he displayed the most cowardly spirit when a maid, a young girl, and bystanders successively linked him to Jesus. Over and over again, he swore, "I don't know that man!" (Matthew 26: 69-73) The honourable thing about Peter is that he acknowledged his weakness and wept. Many Christians can neither realise nor acknowledge their mistakes so quickly as to repent urgently.

We also note that criminals are not always fools or inhuman. There was an incident on the cross shortly before Jesus died. Two robbers had been crucified along with him. While one ridiculed Jesus about his 'assumed godliness', the other took advantage to repent, saying, "...the sentence we have received corresponds to our crimes .... Jesus, remember me when you come into your kingdom" (Luke 23: 39-43). Someone once said that the thief stole the final absolution and earned undeserved access to heaven. However, the robber's statement underlines that it is never too late to repent.

Perhaps the funniest episode occurred at the resurrection of Jesus. The chief priests and Pharisees had deployed stern guards at the tomb so that no one could smuggle the corpse out. However, a grand earthquake shook the earth as "an angel descended from heaven ...rolled back the stone, and sat upon it." The guards fainted and shivered to near death (Matthew 28: 2-4). So why were they deployed at all?

By Venansio Ahabwe, published in Saturday Monitor, 3rd April 2010

25. Why Judas Iscariot is the best Christian

As we conclude celebrations to mark the resurrection of Jesus Christ, let us ask ourselves: Who is the worst man that ever lived in Christian history? Judas Iscariot! Why? He betrayed Jesus!!

Such would probably be the answer from most Christians. Apart from Jesus' tormenters who ultimately crucified him, Judas has been roundly held responsible for the Saviour's death. However, if I was a judge and Judas was brought before me, I would acquit and award him the costs of the case.

A critical look at the role played by Judas Iscariot in the torture and death of Jesus Christ reveals that Judas did not necessarily do a wrong thing. Every Christian agrees that the death of Jesus Christ was primarily a good thing.

The Church teaches that humanity was so wicked that it required an extraordinary sacrifice, and God provided it in the form of Jesus. We would not be celebrating Easter (Christ's resurrection) if he had not died. To think that Judas's 'betrayal' of Jesus was a mistake is to assume therefore that his suffering and death was equally needless and avoidable. It is also to portray Iscariot as a malicious and greedy person who would never have stopped at anything to earn a few pieces of silver –even if it required delivering his best friend to the murderers.

The National Geographic Society in Washington claims that Judas was actually the best friend of Jesus and turned him over to the authorities only because Jesus asked him to. An alleged Gospel of Judas, said to have been disallowed by the early Church because it contradicted the gospels of Matthew, Mark, Luke and John, has indeed opened debate about the level of Judas's impiety. It suggests that Jesus shared with Judas secrets not known by the other disciples. In a key passage, Jesus compares Judas to the other disciples, saying, "You will exceed all of them. For you will sacrifice the man that clothes me." This implies that by helping Jesus get rid of his flesh; Judas would help liberate the divine being within.

In the conventional gospels, it is still evident that Jesus understood that his suffering and death would come, not by human but heavenly design. Long before his crucifixion, he had told his disciples, "The son of man must suffer greatly ... and be killed..." (Luke 9: 22). Peter once tried to persuade Jesus from believing that he would be killed, but Jesus rebuffed him: "You are an obstacle to me. You are thinking not as God does but as human beings do" (Matthew 16: 23).

To blame Judas Iscariot is surely to think 'as human beings do'. Jesus Christ knew he would suffer in Jerusalem. It is wrong to imagine that he was cornered, overpowered and killed by mere humans. He was aware of the entire plot and would have avoided it if he wanted. He actually hints to Pilate that there would have been heavenly intervention if he had not wilfully subjected himself to the worldly authority (John 18: 36 – 37).

Centuries before Judas was born, a prophecy of the life and death of Jesus Christ was made. He would be "spurned ... pierced ... crushed ... harshly treated ... oppressed and condemned ...and cut off from the land of the living ..." (Isaiah 53). A comment from the African Bible says: "This is a description of a sinless servant who by his voluntary suffering ... saves. It is through self-sacrifice ... that he achieves salvation."

The suffering of Jesus Christ was 'voluntary', so Judas personally had nothing to do to prevent it. I think he participated only as God's instrument, having committed all his time and life to Jesus. He acknowledged his mistake; he was remorseful to see Jesus truly dying... "He regretted what he had done ... saying, 'I have sinned in betraying innocent blood' (Matthew 27: 3 – 5).

However, some scholars argue that by handing over Jesus, Judas was simply doing God's will. Steven Patterson, a professor of the New Testament at Eden Theological Seminary in Webster Groves, has thus commented, "If his (Jesus') betrayal was required for the events that followed to occur, isn't he (Judas) more of a hero than a villain?" I strongly agree.

By Venansio Ahabwe, published in The New Vision, Kampala 18th April 2006

26. Respect my right to speak wrong Kiswahili

I have been accused and sentenced to a strange term. My accusers have declared me a Congolese as either a punishment or proof for speaking a diseased breed of Kiswahili, though I have consistently pleaded not guilty. These people should know that the Bongo president has already pronounced himself on the matter of and rejected dual citizenship, so to brand me a Congolese is to place me on a direct collision course with the head of state and in conflict with the law. I do not want to face a police investigation – *ndugu* Alfred Tibaingana is very uncompromising, I hear.

I have been shocked at these wrong, outrageous accusations labeled on me. The first time someone accused me of being a Congolese, I was not sure if it was a crime to be a Congolese in Dar es Salaam, and neither had I observed myself carefully to ascertain if I physically resembled the Congolese.

I have since observed myself many times in a mirror but as soon as I step aside from it, I forget my real appearance. Often, I rely on other people to know whether I am good-looking or an ugly sight, whether I deserve to be loved and respected or hated and despised. I normally look for genuine comments from the new people I encounter; then I return home amused. But I will have to stop this habit since it is proving to be unreliable and dangerous.

On all the previous occasions, I have successfully defended myself that I have never been, I am not, and do not intend to be a Congolese. Interestingly, new charges have always been preferred against me – this time declaring me a Kenyan. Yet again, I have been successful so far, in persuading my accusers that I am not a Kenyan either. What I know for sure is that until the East African boarders are torn down, I will not be anywhere near sharing citizenship with the Kenyans.

The real problem is that I have been unfairly accused for exercising my right to speak wrong, sometimes colloquial Kiswahili. The obvious fact is that my Kiswahili qualifies to pass as the poorest in the whole of Bongo. However, I had never anticipated all this trouble, considering that it is quite uncommon in Tanzania for citizens to be interested in finding out which part of the country the others originate from or what tribe one is. It is just enough to know that one is a Tanzanian.

Yet on my part, the question that refuses to go away is, "Wewe ni kabira gani?" I have been suspecting that perhaps, since the Congolese president is Kabira, it is the reason people think I am a Congolese because they cannot easily tell my *kabila*. I have sworn by my father that I will not declare my *kabila* to anyone because I do not want to breed and promote sectarianism. Pressed hard to declare my *kabila*, I once chose to mention that I belong to the most conspicuous native race in town – the Masai. On hearing this, my interrogators rolled in the dust in a feat of laughter, demanding that I should speak a little Kimasai.

What is disturbing is that when I tell the truth or insert in a simple lie to flavour a conversation, still I am rarely believed. The apparent sectarian attitude against me is fanned by my fluency deficiency in speaking Kiswahili. Yet I must interact with the rest of the waswahili, challenging as it may be.

Folks! I want to make it categorically clear that malicious suspicion and wrongful accusation of an innocent, unarmed civilian is itself a crime and very intolerable indeed from the date of publication of this notice. There is nothing like wrong Kiswahili; only appropriate Kiswahili, simplified to suit specific purposes, in the context of the speaker and the linguistic ability of an individual. People who were lucky to muster the language, as toddlers must not forget to be humble.

Kiswahili is an international language and must be allowed to grow and assume new accents, lexicons, and semantics – the more reason we today have the "Dar city slang". With the adoption of Kiswahili by the African Union and proposals to make it a language of the computer, the East African coastal people have lost the Kiswahili monopoly and must allow it to be sacrificed at the altar of globalisation. For that matter, I am looking for a lawyer to assure me that the accusations against me are human rights violations. Then I will be flying to the International Crimes Tribunal in Arusha to lodge my case. Stand warned.

By Venansio Ahabwe, published in Sunday Citizen, Dar es Salaam 20th October 2004

27. The priest and the mine dog!

Dogs and all beasts in general are not religious. It is not even clear whether they are aware that God exists at all; although we know that he created them. Since animals and humans speak different languages, religious leaders may find it hard to teach the animals about God and his ways. In return, a beast may not tell a priest or sheikh from a lay scamp like Peering Eye.

When religious leaders recently visited Barrick Gold mine, they were chiefly upset that of all the rigorous safety procedures they had endured, some sniffer dogs were unleashed to watch over every step they took to ensure that nothing went wrong. After the visit, the clerics bellowed with fury in protest against the company's discourteous act. How on earth do you suspect a religious chap of villainy and subject them, who represent God here on earth, to a thorough security check?

"We were indeed humiliated. We were treated as if we were common criminals!" said Bishop Hakiah Omindo Deya of the Mara Anglican diocese, shortly after the visit. Subsequently, Barrick Gold Mines denied ever unleashing dogs and heavy arms against religious leaders who had walked into the company uninvited. ('Mine denies humiliating visiting clerics, apologises' *The Citizen* 30th January 2008).

Company spokesman Mr Teweli Teweli apologised for his security guards who left no stone unturned in checking each priest and sheikh for possible weapons of mass destruction. The clerics were also asked to surrender their mobile phones and cameras at the main gate.

In all honesty, Peering Eye believes the security trial which the clerics underwent was neither bad nor humiliating as Bishop Deya thinks. If at all it was humiliating, humility is what we expect of a religious leader. No regrets. Secondly, religious leaders must show the way in the fight against corruption. Why does a priest or sheikh believe that it is okay for a lay person to submit to the rigours of the security machinery at the mining company, and that standard practice should be discarded when the cleric shows up in a robe?

Peering Eye would sympathise with the religious leaders for the misery they suffered only if they were blaming the company for imposing arduous measures against everybody: you and I inclusive. Thirdly dogs, like other beasts have never participated in matters of the temple. You know your cleric because you rely on him for spiritual guidance: he preaches to you, you give him offerings to send to God, you visit each other, and he will preside at your funeral.

It is different for a dog: none of the clerics has ministered to it; they do not ask for its offertory, they are silent when it is mistreated, starved or killed; they do not care where it goes after death – heaven or hell. Therefore, when it is sent to keep security, a dog is impartial to the lay or religious persons. For that reason the dogs of Mara Gold mine must be praised for doing their work.

Perhaps a religious leader might be interested to know that God knows the animals personally and they know him too. Laura J. Parkman has written, "All animals know God. They don't question HIS existence or argue HIS methods. They don't feel the need to improve or change what God has already made perfect. They know God without thinking about it or trying to explain it. They simply know and accept."

What is lacking in this text is that animals know a priest! The only man of God, whom animals ever recognised, was Daniel who was thrown into a lions' den overnight but the fierce beasts refused to have him for their supper (read Daniel 6:4-27). He was in danger of death but did not complain like Bishop Deya and his group.

St. Francis of Assisi, legend says, preached to birds and they surrounded him with interest. He also tamed a deadly wild wolf which he confronted in the hills, called it "brother wolf", and led it into town to the shock of the residents.

The Bongo clerics have never befriended a beast but are sobbing that someone accompanied them with a harmless dog. What a different kind of spiritualists!

By Venansio Ahabwe, published in Sunday Citizen, Dar es Salaam, 3rd February 2008

28. Dog performs a miracle, and saves human life

A deadly person is sometimes abused and accused of showing animal behaviour. This time around, a humane dog has done what is clearly a miracle and has been credited for being more human than a human being.

A baby girl was born in Kenya and thrown away by its mother, a couple of days ago. A family dog went out hunting for food to feed her puppies. She discovered the baby girl aged about two weeks, dumped in a forest near Nairobi. The dog carried the child in her teeth, crossed the road towards the home of its owner and placed the baby beside her puppies. She then lay protectively beside the soiled infant, who was wrapped in a torn black cloth. When some children of that family alerted their mother about the presence of a mysterious crying child on their compound, she hurried and found their dog in possession of the miraculous baby. The fortunate baby, christened Angel by nurses, is now at Kenyatta National Hospital.

Surprisingly, Angel who was rejected and condemned to death by her own mother has generated compassionate emotions across the globe. There are reports of callers from as far as Japan, Venezuela, and South Africa offering not only material and financial support but also homes for the extant baby. Some of the callers have requested to be Angel's adoptive parents.

One wonders how many people today may be angry at the dog's act and would have strongly advised it to mind its own business when it came across the helpless infant. It had its own puppies and they were clearly at the verge of starvation. Indeed it was out to fend for them. The baby would have been a delicious meal for her hungry family. Why could it not save its own first before it could think of taking care of human life? The dog earned herself a good name and unprecedented praise. Newspapers, television channels, radio stations, online publications, and other media around the globe projected it as a kindly creature with exceptional compassion.

Here is a stinging irony. A beast understood that it had a duty to fend for its young ones and ensure that they lived. On the contrary, a human being regarded her own child as sheer garbage, fit to be dumped and rot in the thick of woodland. Many people would certainly have supported the act of the baby-thrower, citing the right of a woman to live a decent life without disturbance from an unwelcome child who must have been conceived by mistake. To what extent many of us consider ourselves as a mistake, perhaps conceived through accident and therefore unworthy of a place on earth remains one of the deep-seated challenges of modern times.

The world is sharply divided into blocs of pro-life and pro-choice activists, the controversy being over abortion especially.

Pro-choice advocates contend that a woman has a right to free herself from the intruder inside her. They say that what she carries in her belly is only a useless object she may get rid of at leisure. It is not a person, with full rights to life. On removal from her body, it may be thrown away. This mentality appears to earn credence as a precursor for population control vis-à-vis the available resources and the need for 'people's improved standards of life'.

This attitude existed in some pre-colonial African societies, where twins were considered an abomination and would be killed at birth. The situation is today exacerbated by the Western influence with the pro-choice fever raging through the United States and Europe. Russia was the first country to legalise abortion in 1920, and it is reported that for every ten Russians born in, there are ten abortions.

Pro-life advocates argue, however, that the right to life must be accorded to everyone, regardless of age, economic conditions, status or wishes of another person. To them, trying to improve one's condition by getting rid of another cannot be justified in any way. They claim that the growing desire to eliminate whomever is considered unwanted is responsible for increased cases of violence, mob justice, child murders, wife beating, wars, slave trade, human trafficking, armed robbery and assassinations.

The wisdom of the pro-choice concept too is becoming increasingly questionable and seems to be backfiring, forcing its authors to eat humble pie. One realises how the re-election of George W. Bush almost solely on the pro-life ticket indicates the direction the Americans are beginning to turn. As for Russia, it is said that an average woman undergoes three abortions in a lifetime, but also that about 13% of Russian women are infertile, owing to complications from many abortions.

What about East Africa? The unnamed dog has exposed and embarrassed us, delivering a miracle, which your proud pastors, self-made miracle workers, are incapable of repeating. Follow the dog's way; care for your children!

By Venansio Ahabwe, published in Sunday Citizen, Dar es Salaam, 22nd May 2005

29. You too can eat a dog and live

Bongo never stops to amaze. Last week on Thursday, Nazir Fazal chastised the Chinese for relishing dog meat at the cost of residents' emotion calm. In his letter titled 'Our dogs ending up on dinner tables', (*The Citizen* 22nd November 2007), the guy lamented the endless demise of Dar es Salaam dogs at the hands of the ravenous Chinese wanderers who savour the taste of this domestic carnivorous, christened dog, that is rampant in our city.

In case you missed his piece, Fazal mourned his Tommy – a dog his family raised to turn into the most ballistic pet ever, only to disappear suddenly one fateful afternoon and the suspects were obvious: the Chinese and their mischievous "sales agents". He accused them of slaughtering, cooking and eating the animals. He thus pleaded, "in view of the gravity of this matter, may I appeal to the Chinese embassy ... to urge its citizens to spare our loving dog ...! It is high time ... the Tanzania Society for the Prevention of Cruelty to Animals and the Tanzania Society Protection and Care of Animals protested ..."

Quite interesting, isn't it? Peering Eye hereby volunteers to respond to Fazal's epistle to the Chinese government on behalf, but without knowledge and consent, of the Chinese embassy. They must be warned nevertheless against distancing themselves from this daring position, or we shall marshal all the dogs in the neighbourhood to launch an attack in order to defend their endangered selves. Moreover, as the letter was published publicly for all to see, we all reserve rights to respond publicly and take positions on this matter.

In the first place, we have grown up not eating dog meat but we do not know really why. We have always eaten a goat, which is the size and stature of a dog. We have eaten a chicken, which is only two-legged unlike a four-legged dog. We have eaten a fish, which is even un-legged – shockingly! Some guys hereabouts have been known to eat a pig, ugly as it looks. We have eaten all sorts of wild and domestic beasts and birds with confidence that it is the right meat to eat. All this time, nobody has protested the killing of an innocent cow, goat, hen, pig, rabbit, or fish – but here comes an animal 'humanist' to contest the eating of a dog. A dog, my foot!

Before we go far, this guy claiming to be sympathetic to animals should be investigated for discrimination; he is favouring some animals and ignoring others when we all know that, like people, all animals are equal. Why should dogs be spared human wrath whereas other harmless animals continue to feed our appetites everyday? For his case to stand, Mr. Fazal is hereby challenged to prove the following: that he does not eat meat at all. If he eats meat, he should state the justification for anyone to eat one animal and refuse to eat another. He should be cross-examined about his source of compassion for dogs and his lack of it for goats and sheep.

The appellant must explain whoever decreed that dogs cannot be eaten while in Dar es Salaam. It is possibly unfortunate that as Peering Eye was growing up, no one introduced him to eating dog meat or he would be happily facing condemnation alongside the Chinese. Are the Chinese forcing anyone to eat dog meat? If they are paying for most of the dogs, are they not supporting the economy? Is the money they are paying for the dogs not used at all to pay some child's school fees?

It should be remembered that while countless goats and cows etc have been slaughtered and eaten, their populations have only grown. In addition, dogs must not become part of our diplomatic relations whatsoever. Since when did a dog deserve such VIP treatment? Should dogs enjoy diplomatic immunity really? No! Think how they pollute your neighbourhood with noise at night ... let us give dog eaters a helping hand – and eat them too.

By Venansio Ahabwe, published in Sunday Citizen, Dar es Salaam 27th November 2007

30. The day I left a Bongoman in tears

The time to check these fraudulent moneychangers has come. They are becoming very many around the city centre. To capture them, the trick is very simple. Get an armed policeman, dress him in a civilian safari suit and send him to the city centre to pretend that he cannot personally trace a forex bureau, and a generous *mbongo* will certainly volunteer to lead him to God-knows-where and attempt to rob his dollars. If the policeman acts before he is beheaded, he will arrest the thug, break the racket and disband the gang!

Well, generous people must be appreciated. Even if you do not to accept a generous person's offer, decency demands that you express your gratitude and add that you are honoured by their kindly gesture, but unfortunately you cannot have any of it.

My Form Two language teacher of always emphasised such civilized British behaviour with his habitual counsel that, when you reject an offer, you say, "No, thank you!"

The good student I thought I were, imagined that I had grasped the point, *kumbe wapi*! I got it in theory and have since failed to put it in practice, despite living in Tanzania, citizens of which can be accused of being 'too full of thanks'. The more the reason I shocked a *mbongo,* who proffered to assist me, and broke into tears that drenched his beard.

It was after a tense week of intense activity and I had ended up at Cine Club in the Mikocheni to celebrate the advent of a weekend. It was expected to be a good weekend consequent upon receiving a US $50 note from Hamis, paying half of his debt to me. As providence had mercifully looked on my wallet, I had to use the miserable shillings to partly wash down the dust that had gathered on my throat during the hectic dry week. After three bottles of Carlsberg, I remained with 600= only.

On Saturday morning, I went to change the dollar note to a more usable legal tender so that I would be at Break Point pub for *mchemusho*. I arrived at *askari* monument, the city centre and jumped out of the *daladala* like a president's guard. I made a few desperate steps towards my favourite forex bureau, Globex Bureau de Change. I neither looked behind nor sideways as I strode across Samora Street, my hand touching the back pocket for my precious wallet while my left hand reached out for the door of the forex bureau shop.

The door was locked. I stopped, in utter incomprehension and evidently troubled. Soon, a youthful kind *mbongo* came forth and offered to help. In his hand was a placard showing exchange rates. He asked if I wished to change some money and I affirmed. The rates were incredibly high. I had expected a rate of shs 1116= but his was 1124= per dollar!

I smiled as he signaled me to the appropriate entrance. He said the premises I was familiar with were currently undergoing renovation, so the business had been shifted to a temporary backdoor room. By now, he had set the trap and I slowly started to walk into it. He volunteered to lead me to the place and was pleased since very many *wabongo* had previously helped me safely get my way in the city on several occasions.

As we walked, I saw that he smiled and was happier than me who was being helped. When we turned towards the back quarters of the building, I noticed I was no longer following one but two people. Yet I saw none of what would be our destination. I made an abrupt stop. The two people ahead of me stopped at once and my initial volunteer asked me what the problem was.

I said I had to retreat briefly and find out if I could get better rates. The man who had not been part of our discussion now stepped forward and laboured to explain that theirs was the best rate in town, adding that they had no intention to cheat me.

"Really", he counselled, "instead of thanking us for trying to help you, you are becoming suspicious!"

He almost went on his knees as he pleaded with me. I observed him closely and realised his eyes were becoming wet. A sweat-like drop escaped his left eye and splashed into his beard.

I made a u-turn at once; my volunteers seemed to hurry towards me. I called on my legs carry me to safety. The volunteers had engaged their *bongo* but I too responded equally like a *mbongo*. I have since seen those placards again and again but I just ignore them.

By Venansio Ahabwe, published in Sunday Citizen, Dar es Salaam, 10th October 2004

31. We do not need more martyrs in Uganda

June 3rd has remained an important day in Uganda ever since the canonisation of the Uganda Martyrs by Pope Paul VI in 1964. It is the day set aside to reflect on the life and fate of the men, Catholics and Anglicans, who were executed for their Christian commitment.

Every year, at such a time, the country is rife with gyrations of celebration in memory of the sons of the soil who triumphed over secularism by shedding their blood. Uganda is said to have produced the biggest number of martyrs worldwide.

However, the attitude of people, at least in Uganda, towards martyrdom is varied. To the majority of the Ugandan Christians, the status of the Uganda Martyrs is enviable. The martyrs were loyal to Jesus Christ to the extent of giving up their lives. Christians believe that it is the martyrs' blood that watered and nurtured Christ's church in Uganda.

The Uganda Martyrs' faith in and love of Jesus Christ were selfless and unreserved. Thus they are really our Christian models, and their actions and behaviour were heroic. Even President Yoweri Museveni, in his address to the Pope, John Paul II in March 1993, appeared proud to welcome him to 'a land that produced African saints'.

On the other hand, some people look contemptuously at the exaltation accorded to the Uganda Martyrs. They regard them as traitors; people who betrayed their African identity and religion, defied their king - Kabaka Mwanga - and embraced a foreign people's magic, thereby degrading their African tradition.

Yet again, not all Christians are unanimous about martyrdom and sainthood. Some Christians, especially of the mushrooming churches, do not recognise the position of the saints in the church. They teach that faith in Jesus Christ is all a Christian needs.

For all intents and purposes, the Uganda Martyrs have significant lessons for Ugandans of all times and walks of life. The circumstances leading to their massacre were shrouded in confusion and violence. It is such violence that Ugandans should deplore, which has hitherto bedevilled our motherland.

This violence, which has characterised our history, is a product of pride, selfishness and highhandedness. Some of the people we look up to as heroes do not deserve that designation; they may be leading tragic lives stemming from their insidious duplicity. In the same spirit, the people we view as traitors or criminals do not actually deserve isolated condemnation. Being on the unpopular side today, they may either represent our society's overall frailty or equally emerge as eventual idols.

When all is said and done, however, we might all have to sympathise and empathise with the men who died as Uganda Martyrs, considering their circumstances. They could have acted out of naivety, ignorance, stubbornness, conscience, or God's design depending on the attitude of each of us towards martyrdom. Otherwise, how come that the missionaries, who presumably understood Christianity much better, often fled for safety whereas their pupils – the new converts - faced danger squarely in the face?

T.S. Eliot, in a play, *Murder in the Cathedral,* expounds martyrdom in the Christian sense.

'*...we do not think of a martyr simply as a good Christian who has been killed because he is a Christian: ...... We do not think of him simply as a Christian who has been elevated to the company of Saints: ... A Christian martyrdom is never an accident..... Still less is a Christian martyrdom the effect of a man's will to become a Saint.... A martyrdom is always the design of God.... never the design of man; for the true martyr is he who has become the instrument of God, who has lost his will in the will of God, and who no longer desires anything for himself, not even the glory of being a martyr.* (Part 1, Interlude: The Archbishop preaches in the Cathedral on Christmas morning, 1170)

From the foregoing, it is apparent that no Christian can or should strive for martyrdom and genuinely be called a martyr, however covertly or overtly devout. Only God appoints His own saintly martyrs from those who surrender themselves completely to Him.

Yet, when God appoints a martyr, it is a man who carries out the mission and kills the martyr. Martyrdom being the design of God, therefore, why do we blame one that kills the person who is destined to become a saintly martyr? In Uganda, for example, the church rejoices in her martyrs – she needed them and the Kabaka, as an agent, killed them.

The problem, however, arises from the fact that whenever vice clashes with virtue, and a virtuous man is destroyed, it provides a serious pointer to the society that what is desired (virtue) is threatened, and everyone should get concerned. The death of martyr indicates that the society's moral fabric needs repair and serious maintenance. It is a warning bell against vice and violence; an invitation to tolerance on the part of the leaders, loyalty on the part of the subjects, ultimately creating harmonious relations with God and one another. The martyred saints are therefore sacrificial models for all.

Uganda has celebrated Martyrs Day for decades but it appears far from having learnt lessons from the martyrs. Vice overshadows virtue, so our country is characterised by violence in form of wars, robbery, torture, injustice, and corruption. All these are heightened by hypocrisy and greed. Uganda needs perfection, not more martyrs.

By Venansio Ahabwe, published in The Monitor, Kampala 3rd June 1998

Part 4: POLITICS AND GOVERNANCE

32. A minister should not earn a salary

If any minister feels they want to earn a salary, let them find out employment opportunities advertised in newspapers, submit applications to the relevant companies and compete with all of us for available vacancies. If they perform well, they will get the job and validly negotiate for any amount of money for their salary, depending on their professional competence and skills.

Then, no one will begrudge them for what benefits they are granted and when and where they might prefer to invest. There is however strong suspicion that government officials do not merely receive hefty wages; they also use their offices to stash away government finances and other resources into personal enterprises.

During a stakeholders' conference held in Dar es Salaam last Tuesday, the Tanzania Centre for Democracy (TCD) Chairman Prof. Ibrahim Lipumba, and companions, urged government to formulate a policy to enable the general public access the lists of public leaders' property. The Comrade thinks this is not necessary.

Who of the TCD partners has disclosed their own properties to anyone in the public? The Comrade is not aware of how much Prof. Lipumba is worth. All of us own properties but everything we have is not necessarily a subject of public scrutiny. People conceal their belongings from public knowledge because of many reasons. They do not want irrelevant people to poke their noses where they should not.

If a person is carrying cash, they do not like the public to know, lest they arouse the interest of wicked or hateful characters and can ultimately pay dearly. At the very least, there is a possibility of inviting alms seekers to you, along with all the attendant inconvenience. No one really wants a destitute for a chief.

Nobody hates a minister that reaps maize, yams, potatoes, avocados, milk, and eggs from his own farm? No one indeed would hate a leader who owns a high-rise building in the city, nor one who manages a successful trading company. The only desire is that the minister should have attained such wealth or property from personal Endeavour, preferably before they were entrusted public resources. They must really not exploit their offices to evade taxation, pilfer the taxpayer's input to the treasury or bring down competitors.

The Comrade argues too that serving in government should be both voluntary and non-paying. When politicians vie for elective offices, they argue that they are anxious and passionate to serve the common man. In view of that, they are not supposed to benefit personally and directly for the services they render for the good of the wretched of the earth.

They never present themselves as wealth-hunters when they vie for government positions. Rather they vow: I want to improve the welfare of my society; I will not rest until the poor have been liberated; I can forfeit anything to ensure that poverty and disease are eliminated. They supposedly are never concerned about their own personal gain but communal welfare. They are willing to sacrifice their own resources to satisfy public need; and they should not demand compensation in return - directly or indirectly.

To crosscheck their transparency though, we do not have to access lists of their property. Rather we should campaign for the removal of the president's and ministers' salaries from the government payroll. Why? While we earn minimally, we pay for our own rent; we pay our own fares and for our medical bills.

For being a minister, on the other hand, one gets a fully serviced and fuelled car; an all-expense paid arrangement wherever they are going: within and out of the country. Falling sick, the minister can access the best Medicare whereas the public foots the bill. There are many advantages associated with a ministerial office, on top of a fat salary. People who are looking for a salary should stay out of government - and corruption will be no more.

By Venansio Ahabwe, published in The Guardian on Sunday, Dar es Salaam, 3rd May 2009

33. A monkey does not set a forest on fire

The Union Parliament Speaker Hon. Pius Msekwa recently warned of the possibility and danger of dirty campaigns that might typify the forthcoming general elections. According to him, however, the problem is not the mere immorality of political rivals adopting smear campaigns of mudslinging, distortion of facts, defamation, and failing to give credit where it is due. Rather, Mr. Msekwa is worried that rivals might exploit the shortcomings of the sitting parliamentarians, reveal their failures to the voters and, ultimately, jeopardise the incumbents' chances of re-election.

He pointed out that dirty campaigns are targeted at the current members of parliament who are often accused of doing very little to cause development in their respective constituencies. Hon. Msekwa said that the serving legislators should be neither blamed for the development lapses in the constituencies they represent nor criticised for being inactive in parliamentary debates. He added that people should shun politicians who go round talking negatively of incumbent members of parliament ('Msekwa hits out at dirty campaigns', *The Citizen* Tuesday 5th July 2005).

With all due respect to the *mheshimiwa* speaker, I desire to disagree with and blame him for discouraging us from bringing incompetent parliamentarians to book. When inefficient members of the national legislative assembly are evaluated to determine if they indeed are meeting the expectations of their constituents, the speaker has no point getting anxious or upset about it. Conversely, it should please him that the voters are interested in electing vibrant, sharp-witted representatives who can never snore in Parliament and are development oriented, because this country desires nothing but development. It should be politically dangerous for members of parliament who win elections but fail to perform to the voters' expectations. Their victory at polls should be a mere flash in the pan.

The absence of development initiatives coupled with a legislator's ineptness in parliamentary debates is the living proof of the legislator's incompetence. Such members of the house are fit for nothing; they should be winnowed out of the national assembly at the next elections, given that it is practically impossible for the ordinary electorate to recall their representatives once the elections are over. A parliamentarian's performance is measured from his participation in the development programmes in the constituency and the country at large. He is not merely a bringer of development but a participant and often a leader in the development process. His success is also ascribable to the quality of debate he puts up in parliament, failure at which must never go unpunished. No responsible citizen should be expected to cheer a parliamentarian who has failed to deliver.

The public has a duty to scrutinise the leaders they elect, so criticism should be regarded as part of the public effort to bring the parliamentarians to account. Anyone who opts for a public office accepts responsibility, which in turn goes with accountability. Moreover, the candidates at elections are never coerced to make promises to the voters whom they give the impression that they would cause amazing progress. The candidates on their own volition make such promises during the campaigns, therefore if they are sure it is not their duty to bring about the stated progress, then they are either elected on the strength of their lies or on the basis of their ignorance of the tasks before them.

Tell us Pius, if the promised development does not come, who should be blamed? What crime does a political rival commit to remind the voters that the person they elected was not equal to the task? To say that the failures of bona fide members of parliament should not be discussed is a rude joke and conjures up memories of sleeping parliamentarians whose duty is simply to sign for hefty salaries and allowances for doing nothing. No matter how much their shortfalls may be covered up, once they are real, everyone is guaranteed to know them soon or late, and when stated as exact facts that they are, it may be misconstrued as malicious mudslinging. Yet in reality, you would think the parliamentarian in question would have the courtesy to apologise and resign.

Parliament is the country's vastest melting pot, whereby a slumbering member robs it of its intended diversity from which to blend national interests, to mould a national outlook. Defeating an incompetent parliamentarian at the subsequent elections would redound to the wakefulness of the constituents about their rights and duties in the development and democratic set-up. When a monkey pleads for a forest not to be set ablaze, it has no reason to give to preserve the jungle, only that it is a familiar dwelling. Similarly Msekwa is simply infatuated with the familiar faces in Parliament.

By Venansio Ahabwe, published in Sunday Citizen, Dar es Salaam 17th July, 2005

34. Give corruption medals!

This is my humble contribution to the commendable crack by the country's Prevention of Corruption Bureau (PCB) to stave the profusion of white collar fraud that slowly but surely is sinking the nation to the base of public paucity. It is only amazing that the battle against corruption is executed with plain favouritism and little motivation. It is small time swindlers that can be pursued with ease.

Suddenly, however, the PCB drags to court a titanic fish in the name of a prominent diplomat that allegedly fleeced the motherland of millions of Euros. Add to this, ongoing investigations by Britain's Serious Fraud Office (SFO), to verify claims that other millions of dollars were paid in bribes to secure the controversial Watchman radar system for Tanzania, whose cost, the World Bank says, was more than four times its real value.

I say Bravo nduguni! The country's corruption rank is incessantly growing. It is high time we awarded medals to the particular luminaries causing this growth. They are not ordinary burglars or common thieves. They have reputations, derived from the lofty bureaus they govern, and must be appropriately recognised, even in disgrace. The better the job one holds or the closer to state power one is, the greater access they have to the national coffers. This also determines the size of the money they can steal, moreover with official power.

Stealing public funds or indeed private property has got many dimensions. 'Need' is one of them. Some people steal money because they actually are in dire need. The man is dragged to court and risks imprisonment because like you and me, the family or other demands forced him to steal money. The second aspect is 'exposure' to the resources.

The corrupt do not just loot nothing, nowhere. They steal the money because it is there, exposed. Other than being protectors of their own wealth, people want their wealth protected from them. At home, you keep away attractive items from children not because they are thieves but they might be tempted to help themselves from bare valuables. Does government ensure that taxpayers' treasures are securely kept or does it knowingly entrust it to the fraudulent?

The third cause of corruption is security. Some people steal money as a way of saving it from being stolen by others. They know that if they do not take it, someone else will. You might pick money by the roadside because you know that whoever may come after you will neither leave it for its real owner to recover nor declare that they ever came across it at all. If caught with the money, you might argue that you neither grabbed the owner's purse nor broke into his house.

The fourth, albeit unintended, reason for corruption is free publicity. A person can steal to make a name. You grab some billion shillings and are caught. You become a centre of public interest: your pictures are displayed in the newspapers free of charge, and stories are written of your birth, upbringing, schooling, and career. A rare opportunity! Your columnist had not heard of and never desired to know this country's ambassador to Italy until he was accused of fraud.

Yet in executing corrupt schemes, it is only money that suffers. No one is harmed in the due course; no one is shot and thus no need for police to pursue the thief with guns. Fuel is saved as are government bullets that might kill or alarm the public.

Corruption sometimes serves as a way of reallocating and making good use of public resources. Money is lying idle in the treasury and Peering Eye lays hands on it, walks off and erects a high-rise edifice in Kariakoo which any member of the public would be at liberty make use of. Think of the resulting social and economic progress.

The Bible say says 'we all have sinned and fallen short of God's grace'. You too have stolen sometimes: a pen in class or a coin on the street. The other day, I was in a bank and a nice guy smiled at me as he asked for my pen, only to disappear with it. Was it his intention to come to the bank and snatch my pen? Where is PCB?

By Venansio Ahabwe, published in Sunday Citizen, Dar es Salaam, 28th January 2007

35.   Mkapa was singing from a wrong hymnbook!

President Benjamin Mkapa (Ben) recently entertained the Ugandan Parliament as he chanted about "the quest for a new governance paradigm for Africa". He was delivering a speech during his farewell state visit to Uganda as President of the United Republic of Tanzania. The Ugandan press copiously described Ben's speech as "powerful" (The New Vision) and "peppered with intellectual overtones" (Daily Monitor). However, Peering Eye viewed it as a vain plea with the legislators to mull over an affair that has long been settled.

I mean, Ben's exhortations were just too late to serve any useful purpose. His wise counsel came quite behind schedule. In fact, Bukoli North MP, Hon. Patrick Mwondha, suggested that Ben had withheld his wisdom till it was too late. "I wish you had visited us a week ago … my colleagues would have picked a leaf from your wisdom," said the frank parliamentarian.

Again, the retiring President of Bongo plainly overstretched Uganda's welcome. It is not a visitor's job to volunteer lessons to his host about family management, in total disregard of the realities in the home visited. Ben's tongue was so inciting that he if he had attempted to address a public rally, police would have characteristically dispersed it with brutal force. If the Parliament he addressed were a radio station, it would have been closed forthwith.

Only shortly had the parliamentarians, in their wisdom, mutilated the country's constitution, on the understanding that out of the twenty-six million citizens of that country, there is only one man with a vision. The vision to lead the country! Then from some space comes Ben urging them to believe that there can be "a shared national vision". The host President himself had pointed out earlier that he would be unwilling to leave the political stage because he saw nobody among Ugandans who had a vision to lead the country.

One politician, named Kizza Besigye, had claimed he had the vision to lead that country, but he has since lived in exile. The current Vice President Prof. Gilbert Bukenya too had once admitted to a local radio that "there are many credible people" in Uganda who could lead the country. When he saw it in a newspaper, he thought it ought to have been a bad dream. He apologised, adding that if at all he had surely claimed that there possibly could be other credible leaders in the country, then Museveni was just "incredibly credible".

Ben's moral view that democratic governance in Africa can only take root if leaders groom potential successors to the presidency was another joke. "Identify potential leaders early," he shouted into the microphone. Please Ben! An African successor is an heir, only desired when the family head is departed. To name one is to invite bad lack; an early death. But when you are becoming strong and wiser the older you grow, why an heir?

Such wisdom, which comes with age, makes a man understand his mission better than others as time goes by. For Ben to say, "create systems ... that are strong ... capable of outliving their founders", was to scorn Museveni's intellect. How could a pot outlive its maker? Will the earth outlive God?

Come to retiring. Ben boasted, "In my ten years as President of the United Republic of Tanzania ..."! How many years? Ten? The Ugandan MPs must have been horrified to see a President who has been in power for a mere decade singing joyfully about retiring from State House. How does one rejoice over a demotion? The argument that is winning hearts in Uganda today is: a good leader should be utilised exhaustively. A constitution can be restrained to mollify human desires.

Methinks Mr. Mkapa picked a wrong hymnbook and sang Chinese, which the press reported, "drew cheers from MPs, discomfort on minister's faces and a smile from President Museveni".

By Venansio Ahabwe, published in Sunday Citizen, Dar es Salaam, 4th September 2005

36. It is African solidarity in crime!

The 15th African Union (AU) Summit has just ended in Kampala with a theme, Maternal, child health and development'. The high point of the summit was nonetheless not bout maternal or child health but perhaps about two other issues – the recent Kampala twin bombings and the indictment of the Sudanese president by the International Criminal Court (ICC).

The threat of the al Shabaab militants has lately spiraled beyond Somalia causing the Kampala tragedy of 11th July 2010, where about eighty soccer fans perished as they watched the World Cup finals. Many international heavyweights from America and Europe turned up at the summit and expressed sympathy for the victims of the bombings as well as support for peacekeeping troops in Somalia.

The United States and United Kingdom representatives said little, if anything, related to the theme of the summit. Their interest lay elsewhere: 'fighting and defeating terrorism' in Somalia. Interestingly, they all seemed unbothered about state inspired terrorism in Africa as we shall see below.

While the AU chairman Dr Bingu wa Mutharika of Malawi, like other leaders at the summit, praised South Africa for successfully hosting the

World Cup, he also poured scorn on the ICC for issuing an arrest warrant for the Sudanese president, Omar al Bashir. In 2009, the ICC declared Mr. Bashir a wanted man, accusing him of committing war crimes and crimes against humanity during his government's military campaign to stem the insurgency in the country's vast region of Durfur.

In June 2010, the ICC expanded the catalog of accusations to include genocide too, and still calls on governments to help arrest the indicted president and hand him over for prosecution since the court does not have a police force to enforce the detention. The arrest warrant still hangs on Bashir's head.

At the opening of the Kampala AU summit where Bashir was conspicuously absent, Dr Bingu asserted that the ICC erred to issue an arrest warrant against a sitting head of state because such an action 'violates the principle of African solidarity and state sovereignty'. Here lies Africa's problem! Where is 'African solidarity' really? Is it solidarity in crime?

The Comrade wanted to call Dr Bingu aside and explain that all animals are equal and none is more equal than others. It is not right that any man should commit crimes with impunity and expect 'brotherly solidarity' simply because he is a 'sitting head of state'. This was the state of affairs in the past and African despots will continue to derive inspiration to wreak injustice and suffering on wananchi without taking liability. They will continue to cling to power if that is what can save them from accountability.

When Dr Bingu proclaimed that the ICC was wrong to ask President Bashir to account, delegates at the summit cheered thunderously. They clapped joyfully 'in solidarity with Bashir'. This was a sad moment! Many citizens of Sudan in the Durfur region have been dehumanised and subjected to the mayhem of displacement, homelessness, poverty, starvation, disease, and death. They are citizens of the Sudan, Africa and world. They were born naked like any delegate that clapped hands when their suffering was implied at the AU summit. One of the suffering citizens would be occupying Bashir's office and him a mere mwananchi who would not like to suffer as they have suffered.

The problem is that our leaders believe that they have all rights to live in splendour while ordinary folks can face all the suffering and that is okay. Kenyan novelist, Ngugi wa Thing'o once argued that whenever anyone is degraded and humiliated, all of us are degraded and humiliated because this is about human beings. If the AU delegates clapped their hands for the suffering people of Durfur, they were celebrating the suffering of all Africans about whom respective governments feel threatened.

Therefore, they clapped for rigging of elections and the ensuing bloodbath in Kenya. They clapped for the endless murders in the Democratic Republic of Congo. They clapped for the toppling of democracy in Zimbabwe. They clapped for the brutalisation of opposition politicians in Uganda. All this is state inspired terrorism. If occasion demanded, the delegates would clap for the murder of albinos - if they were a threat to the 'sitting head of state' – and express solidarity in crime.

By Venansio Ahabwe, published in Guardian on Sunday, Dar es Salaam, 31st July 2010

37. Will Kenya become East Africa's democratic model?

The fact that Kenya held a peaceful referendum in a free and fair election shows that greatness does not lie in never falling at all but in rising up every time we fall. Kenya is a country with a tattered international image as a result of the 2007 general elections in which Mr Emilio Mwai Kibaki was dubiously declared winner of that year's presidential polls. His nemesis, Raila Odinga promptly disputed Kibaki's victory, rousing his fretful supporters to stage protests that soon degenerated into violent rampage, directed at Kibaki's followers, especially members of his clan living outside their traditional homeland.

At the same time, Kibaki's loyalists retaliated by attacking the groups that favoured Raila Odinga's candidature, especially the Luo and Kalenjin. The conflict, which was primarily of political nature, shortly assumed a tribal slant. Attacks and counterattacks led to destruction of more than thirteen hundred lives as well as loss of vast amounts of property. Kenya has since endured the scandalous ignominy of ethnic bigotry that arose at a time when East Africa was steadily advancing towards a borderless region and the world rolling into a global village.

Three years down the road, however, the same country has conducted what can be rated as the most competitive but peaceful, free and fair election in Africa. During the campaigns and voting process, members of the same government campaigned on opposing sides of the debate.

As a cabinet Minister for Higher Education, Mr William Ruto did not fear to follow his conscience and provide leadership to the 'no' camp that rallied Kenyans to reject the proposed constitution. He was not harassed for doing that.

He was treated with respect, regardless of occasional strategic jabs that go with political campaigns.

When the 'no' camp lost the vote, Mr Ruto graciously conceded defeat on behalf of his camp, and promised that the points of contention could be resolved during the implementation phase. Daniel Arap Moi, the former President, campaigned on the 'no' side but his rallies were not dispersed with teargas. Religious leaders spoke out strongly against parts of the proposed constitution but they were not attacked.

Your columnist has witnessed campaigns in Uganda where anyone that does not agree with President Museveni can easily be blocked from campaigning, harassed by police and military forces, branded a terrorist or a criminal of sorts, or arrested. This is possibly happening elsewhere in Africa. The new constitution approved a few days ago can be seen as a deliberate effort by Kenyans to throw away the country's corrupt and violent past and face the future with a fresh standing.

This is a mark of a dynamic society. It was an honourable step by President Mwai Kibaki; possibly the best gift he has given his nation. He has just done his part. The only thing The Comrade wants him to do is to relinquish his office and allow an opportunity for another Kenyan to become President and implement the new constitution.

You do not want the Ugandan experience where someone excites the population with a constitution during his nascent days in government. When the same constitution seems to stand in his way, however, he tears it down to advance his private interests.

In 2005, President Yoweri Museveni of Uganda engineered a constitutional amendment by bribing the gutless members of parliament with five million shillings each, to remove Presidential term limits from the country's supreme law, to allow him stay in power till death. Uganda adopted a new constitution in 1995 at a time when President Museveni would have been bowing out of office. The constitution, he believed, was his personal initiative and thus no one could understand how to implement it. So he had to stay on and on and on and on!

One hopes that President Mwai Kibaki does not become such a good student of East Africa's strongman that rules Uganda. If he does, Kenya will have wasted resources coming up with a new constitution. When all is said and done, however, the country with the most despised democratic record may suddenly become East Africa's democratic model.

By Venansio Ahabwe, published in Guardian on Sunday, Dar es Salaam, 8th August 2010

38. Rev Mtikila should give to Caesar what is Caesar's

A story is told of a man whose car broke down near a monastery and he sought help from the resident monks. Although he was not a monk himself, the monks fixed his car, fed and comforted him till he left. While he stayed at the monastery, he heard a strange sound, knowledge of which was only reserved for monks. What was the sound? You will know shortly.

Let us assume that President Jakaya Mrisho Kikwete was the man in need of help and Rev John Mtikila the monk. Would the monk really provide the desired help to a man who is not merely a stranger but even more gravely not a monk? Recently, the chairman of the Democratic Party Rev Mtikila authored an epistle about the alleged 'bad intentions of President Kikwete against Christianity' ('Police interrogate Mtikila over controversial circular' *The Guardian,* 16th April 2010).

The Comrade believes strongly that a reverend should precisely lead a church not a political party, in the first place. In church, he can directly tell God to intervene politically if he believes that God is interested in political matters. A comedian Jay Leno once said that 'if God wanted us to vote, he would have given us candidates'. You doubt, however, if God really is the giver of the foul political leaders we have in Africa.

The concept of democracy and voting must have been a human innovation, possibly with divine inspiration, and we cannot hold God responsible for the inherent flaws that go with the enterprise that is clearly secular. Politics is called a dirty game where every saintly person would find no interest to play a role, like an immaculately clad person would not take a seat on a blatantly smeared bench.

As regards political representation, it is both hard and needless that every religious group should have a president from within their ranks all at the same time. Most citizens in Bongo subscribe to some form of religious conviction. Yet if anyone should assume the country's presidency, they are obliged to serve the entire population with without favour. This is perhaps where Rev Mtikila might have a point, supposing he is saying the truth and has evidence to back up his allegations against Mr Mrisho.

To *The Comrade,* however, religious convictions of any particular individual, even if he were a president, mean nothing. Many people today crisscross the religious field but conversions are not dependant on the president's perceptions. You do not abandon your religion simply because you have been elected president of a secular republic, nor does an ordinary citizen thrust aside his religious inclinations simply because the man in power may not subscribe to it.

A good president is one who tries to be nondenominational without abandoning his own faith. Yet the godliest president is him who can discern that people are variously endowed and free to pursue their personal convictions, including religion. No president, even if it were Rev Mtikila himself, should imagine that he is possibly nearer to God than an ordinary bloke like your columnist.

Shouting about God, Christianity, Islam and blah-blah does not actually mean that we are building a godly nation. Ironically, godliness seems to thrive better in secular conditions than where everyone wears religion on their sleeves not as a sign of humility but pomp and arrogance. Religious enthusiasts should submit to political authority, knowing that to do so is to proclaim the superiority of heavenly sovereignty.

When the Nazarene advised people to give to Caesar what belongs to Caesar (Matthew 22: 21), he possibly wanted to teach them the virtue of humility – and stress the timeless intercourse between religion and politics. Heavenly matters, though superior to earthly matters, do not abolish them. His other probable lesson was that spiritual matters are far above secular ones, thus to compare the two was to inadvertently equate them and, in the end, deprive the former of its worthy supremacy. So what was the strange sound at the monastery, knowledge of which was reserved for monks? You cannot know because you are not a monk!

By Venansio Ahabwe, published in Guardian on Sunday, Dar es Salaam, 25th April 2010

39. The UK can learn Africa's political tricks, if nothing else.

On Thursday 6 May 2010, the United Kingdom held puzzling general elections across 650 constituencies. Puzzling because none of the participating political parties won, as none attained the 326 seats needed for an overall majority! It means that the country would neither have a Prime Minister nor a government.

While David Cameron's Conservative Party won the largest number of votes and parliamentarians, it still fell short of the desired majority by twenty seats, culminating into a hung parliament. The ruling Labour Party had an opportunity to stay in power through a coalition government with the Liberal Democratic Party where the incumbent Gordon Brown would still be Prime Minister. However, Mr Brown suddenly announced his resignation from the job, leaving the opposition's David Cameron to ascend the coveted office with Liberal Democrat, Nick Clegg, as his deputy.

Mr Brown knew that as the British could not give him and his party a majority vote, they expressed their dissatisfaction with his regime and it was only sensible that he listened to their message and abided by their verdict. This is the decency that we crave for in Africa; when and whether it will ever come, The Comrade knows not!

As the above developments emerged, Ugandan President Yoweri Museveni held a press conference at State House in Entebbe where he expressed shock about the conduct and results of the elections in the United Kingdom. He wondered why any election could not produce a winner, resulting into a Hung Parliament.

"The electoral commission in the UK is very inefficient," Museveni carped. However, "we do not go lecturing people and issuing reports on that. In the UK, people are rioting on the streets; no one has won," he said.

President Museveni's attack originated from recent reports that the United Kingdom and the United States were critical of the electoral system in Uganda where the president tends to manipulate processes with corruption and intimidation to ensure that he does not lose power. The US Secretary of State, Hilary Clinton, recently presented a report to Congress noting that as Uganda prepares for general elections due next year, it is clearly far below international election standards. The report indicated that ongoing voter registration was poorly organised; the electoral commission is dependent on the whims of the president; a key part of the work of the Uganda police is to harass opposition politicians, and radio stations cannot host opposition campaigners without risks of having their licences withdrawn or individual journalists penalised.

The opposition has thus been calling for a situation where the country can have free and fair elections, generally acceptable to all political players. Amidst all these, the biggest beneficiary of flawed processes believes established democracies deserve nothing but contempt. When President Museveni poured scorn on the British electoral developments, he possibly meant that they should have consulted African leaders about the best way to conduct polls. Go to Kampala, Harare, Tripoli, Nairobi, and Addis Ababa.

In the course of tallying the 2005 general elections in Ethiopia, the Prime Minister declared a state of emergency. He outlawed public gatherings, assumed direct command of the security forces, and replaced the capital city police with federal police and Special Forces drawn from elite army units. The national election board of Ethiopia (NEBE) also decided to stop the vote tallying process, an act which was not rescinded for nearly a week. In the end, more than 60,000 people were arrested, about 200 killed in the ensuing chaos, and almost 800 injured. Yes, the Prime Minister had to stay in office.

In 2006, Uganda's leading opposition candidate Dr Kizza Besigye enjoyed soaring popularity. He returned from exile as the electoral commission had just started registering new voters. Registration centres, which were literally abandoned suddenly came to life with queues of excited punters most of them apparently buoyed by Dr Besigye's return. As more and more people turned up for registration, the exercise was quickly stopped in spite of widespread protests. To curb this growing support for a political opponent, Dr Besigye was arrested, charged with rape and kept in prison for almost the entire campaign period. Yes, the President had to stay in power.

The most recent elections in Kenya and Zimbabwe produced identical results: the incumbent presidents clearly lost the polls but only allowed the winners to play second fiddle as Prime Ministers. All these anomalies arise from 'African tricks' that Europeans are ignorant of. That is why President Museveni doubted the electoral processes of the UK. His message seems to be, "if there is nothing good to learn from us, simply learn from us what we are best at!"

By Venansio Ahabwe, published in Guardian on Sunday, Dar es Salaam, 6th June 2010

40. Stealing on the behalf of the people

On Good Friday, Bishop Methodius Kilaini advised looters of all respects, especially national plunderers, to apologise for their misdeeds and seek God's exculpation. As though God's absolution was not enough, Kilaini added that all those "implicated in the looting of public funds should be made to refund the stolen money" (see: 'Bishop wants loot recovered' *The Citizen* 22nd March 2008).

As of now, no one has confessed to stealing taxpayers' money as bishop Kilaini has requested. But what if the looter gave the money to the church? Peering Eye knows that to discuss corruption in Africa (or Bongo) is to open a Pandora's Box. The people who steal public money are so empowered socially and politically that a casual analyst can easily pay the price for citing the facts about fraud.

This is a democratic country and neither the bishop nor Peering Eye is expected to take a standpoint that is not supported by the people. Once upon a time, the potent leader of Zimbabwe called a referendum over the issue of land redistribution in that country. Robert Mugabe was certain the majority Africans who had been dispossessed of their land since colonial times would eagerly support the land reform programme. However, the landless Zimbabweans voted against owning and managing land as though to say: the whites are managing it on our behalf.

Was bishop Kilaini aware of this incident that had occurred in Tanzania's backyard? Well, Peering Eye fears to antagonise a man of God but since religion is supposed to help us become honest and truthful, let us prophesy from practical experience. In a near future, a referendum (a campaign where citizens are asked decide on an important question through a vote) will occur. The Bongo public will decide on the question of corruption by supporting either the bishop or the politicians, including those implicated in the corruption scandals.

The bishop will campaign against graft in public offices and call for holiness as central tenet in human existence and transaction of everyday business while the politicians will counter that there can never be meaningful development if citizens become generally meek and holy. The politicians will also invoke the takrima memories and utilise the booty to grease the palms, throats as well as stuffing wabongo tummies to swing public opinion in their favour. They will win, the bishop will be derided and he will find it hard to minister to his flock after a vote of no confidence at the referendum polls!

If Peering Eye could be one of the scandalous folks i.e. the men who steal government money, here below is the speech he would deliver to cheering crowds at the rallies across the country. He would say:

Fellow citizens, I stand before you as a humble, innocent civilian to argue my case in the court of public opinion. Fortunately, you are the judges in that noble court. If you convict me, my dear comrades, I will be prepared to serve the undeserved sentence you prescribe. If you find me innocent and acquit me, I will applaud your wise judgement and lead you in a victorious procession to the doorsteps of the church to proclaim to the bishop how wicked he is and what he must repent of. I know already what lies deep in your hearts: you all want me acquitted.

Ladies and Gentlemen, I would add, I invite you to stand with me in these trying moments and to be my witnesses. I have dedicated all my life to the welfare of our motherland. Some people think that this mass of a belly I am tolerating is a result of corruption. On the contrary, it has arisen from starvation; I miss meals as I worry about the future welfare for you and your children. Do you call that corruption? It is the man who talks about corruption who is possibly corrupt. Stealing or not, you elected me, not the bishop, and I do everything in your name. Oh yeah!

By Venansio Ahabwe, published in Sunday Citizen, Dar es Salaam 20th April 2008